If You Weren't Here
This Would Not Be Happening

plogs from my life

Life is either a daring adventure or nothing.

—*Helen Keller*

If You Weren't Here
This Would Not Be Happening

plogs from my life
by Walter G. Meyer

MaxM LTD.

If You Weren't Here, This Would Not Be Happening
plogs from my life

First Printing November 2020

Print ISBN   978-0-9825132-7-9
eBook ISBN   978-0-9825132-8-6

Book design by David Maxine
Cover photo by [XPOZD]

www.waltergmeyer.com

MaxM Ltd.

Photo on page 1: "Lighthouse, Bahia de Los Angeles, Baja California, Mexico."
Photo on title page spread: "Venice Pier at Sunset."
Photo on dedication page: "A man on the rocks above the Pacific Ocean in Michoacán, Mexico."

IF You Weren't Here is dedicated to all of those with whom I have shared life's adventures--those moments, happy and sad that have helped make my life fascinating. And to all of those who read and commented on these memories as I posted them on my Facebook page during the COVID-19 isolation spurring me to collect them into this book. I am glad I could entertain you and myself with these stories of my crazy life.

If you weren't here, these moments would not have meant as much.

I wrote these stories to distract myself during the time of the COVID-19 shutdown and posted them, a story a day, on Facebook to entertain my friends and followers. A few people have asked me if all of these stories are true. Yes. I have a weird life, what can I say? I'm not a clever enough writer to invent some of the craziness I have lived. Where possible, I have included photos of some of the incidents as a way of saying, yes, this really happened—proof that I am not making this shit up. Over the course of the more than 250 stories I posted on Facebook, someone said they were too long to be normal posts, but weren't really blogs so I coined a new term—plog—for my posts that morphed into blogs.

What follow are memories. Snippets of my life. Like any incident in which other people are involved, their memories of those same events may be different from mine, but these were the way these moments stuck in my mind and influenced my life.

Some of these incidents served as the inspiration for parts of books or screenplays or stage plays I have written, or will the basis for scenes in projects I plan to write, but what is recorded in this volume are the actual stories the way they happened before I fictionalized them for other purposes.

The title of the book comes from the time I was in the middle of a shoot-out in Washington, D.C. A friend and I were covering our heads, cowering on the floor of his car as bullets whizzed around the intersection in front of us. My friend looked at me and said, "If you weren't here, this would not be happening! Shit like this only happens when you're around!" That wasn't exactly true: he got robbed at gunpoint three times in D.C., and I wasn't with him during any of those holdups. I'm quite happy to say I've never been robbed at gunpoint. There was that time I was pickpocketed in Paris, but that is a story for another time.

On one of my infrequent visits to Philadelphia, the train on which I was riding got shot at. Of the hundreds of people who got off the train, the local news chose me to interview, much to the consternation of friends who rode that train every day and weren't questioned. Almost every year when I go to San Diego's City Hall to watch the election returns, I get interviewed by the local news. Why I am singled out of the

My appearance on Jeopardy! *in 1987. Yes, I was as nervous as I looked. The photo was taken off a television by a photographer for the* Pittsburgh Press *to accompany an article I wrote about my experience.*

hundreds of people in the room, I don't know. On the rare times when it doesn't happen, I wonder why.

For most of these stories I have changed the names of people. They have a right to their privacy and these are my stories, not theirs. They can write their own books. I have kept the names of celebrities because in most cases, who they are is the point of the story. But in some cases, I have obscured their names to cover for their misdeeds or to protect their privacy as well.

Strange things do tend to happen when I am around, and at least part of that comes from the number of diverse jobs I have had. The parents of a fellow writer lived in the same retirement community as my parents in Pittsburgh. One day I ran into the friend's dad and he asked me, not unkindly, when his son and I were going to get "real jobs." His son has been much more successful than I have been in my career, with over a dozen published books, and having worked as editor-in-chief of major magazines. But somehow, that wasn't real enough for a father who had spent his year in a corporate office job.

Likewise, my father, who spent 44 years behind a desk at a bank, was asking me when I was going to get a real job until shortly before he died. But an interesting thing happened after he died. At the funeral home when I introduced myself to friends of his whom I had never met before, they replied, "Oh, you're the writer in California! Your father bragged about you all the time!"

That day in the retirement community, the proper response to my friend's father occurred to me. I said that I figured out that at least in my case, being a writer was sort of like being an alcoholic. I realized that I would probably be more successful in life, have more money, have more stable relationships and be less stressed if I could just quit. But I can't. And my life has been happier since I stopped fighting who I needed to be, on a few different fronts, but more of that in coming chapters.

Over the years I have worked a variety of jobs while trying to support my writing habit. I was a clerk/messenger for a law firm. I taught racquetball and managed a racquet club. I worked night audit at a ski resort. I taught comedy traffic school. I was a manager at the world's first phone-in, drive-thru supermarket. I was assistant manager of a bookstore and of a motel. I was a production assistant on a low-budget TV show. I did some acting and modeling. I ran my own business selling framed postage stamps. I worked for a nonprofit that helped people find jobs. I have done public relations both freelance and on staff at a couple of places. I've worked as a tour guide and I have taught people to work polling places. I managed an archive. I have learned from each of these jobs and they provided threads for the interesting tapestry of my life.

Many of my writing assignments have also led to adventures and meeting fascinating people. In addition to the books I've written about Alzheimer's disease, baseball, business and sales, leadership, yoga and prison, I have written articles about celebrities, the Navy, sea turtles, pawn shops, Zambonis, travel destinations, history, football, fire insurance, and how to buy a man's suit, all of which gave me new experiences and made me what my father often called "a storehouse of useless information." I would argue with him that it wasn't all useless; my breadth of knowledge got me on the popular TV game show *Jeopardy!* And I wrote about that experience as well.

I've had a lot of people tell me that I'm one of the most interesting people they've ever met. I'm not sure I am that interesting, just that interesting things do tend to happen around me. I was once selected by a library to be a "human book" to be "checked out" by anyone who wanted to hear my story.

I once had a friend tell me, "You collect interesting people the way other people collect interesting stamps." Unique individuals seem drawn to me whether on an airplane or in bars or even just on the street.

Case in point. A friend and I were walking down a street in West Hollywood when we heard someone call out, "On your left, please, gentlemen!" We stepped aside just as a speeding bicyclist whizzed by us. On the rear rack of his bike, he had made a holder specifically the size of a 12-pack and it he had a half-case of beer. I jokingly yelled, "Hey, that will cost you a beer!"

The guy on the bike hit his brakes so hard he laid rubber on the concrete. He came to an immediate halt and dismounted his bike so abruptly I thought he was going to come back and punch me for being a smart ass. Instead, he ripped open the package, pulled out two cans of beer, and held them out to my friend and me, saying, "I can't believe that's what it costs to ride down a sidewalk in West Hollywood these days!" Before we could even react, the guy had remounted his bike and took off.

My friend looked at the beer in his hand and then at me and said, "This is on you. Shit like this only happens to you."

Even how I met that friend was random. I was on the front porch of a cabin I was sharing with friends in Guerneville on the Russian River in Northern California when he was walking by. I said hello. He said hello. I invited him in for a drink. We have been friends ever since.

I was at a Renaissance Faire and a random 15-year-old boy approached me and started talking to me. That was over 20 years ago. Now he has a wife and two children and we are still friends. He and I have dinner whenever his business brings him to San Diego.

I met a teen in a juvenile traffic school class. By the end of class, he had adopted me as his surrogate uncle. Over 20 years later, we are also still friends. He and his wife live in the San Francisco Bay area. He recently hired me to do a little project for him, so you never know how things will come around.

Somehow people trust me. Whether on airplanes, in bars or while I was interviewing them for something I was writing, I have numerous people start sentences, "I have never told anyone this, but..."

Indeed, I am still friends with many of the people I met on an airplane or at a hotel bar. One such airport encounter was with a couple who were retiring from New York City to San Diego. We stayed in touch, and at one point, I introduced her to a friend of mine. The woman thought my friend looked familiar. Turns out, she remembered him from their neighborhood in Brooklyn. His brother and her brother had been best friends in high school almost 50 years earlier.

In addition to all the strange things that happen to me, I always seem one degree of separation removed from major events and people. (See Section VI: Six Degrees from Gettysburg.) I knew someone who kissed Adolph Hitler. I met a woman who worked with Winston Churchill and knew cousins of Franklin Roosevelt's. I knew the guy who streaked the Academy Awards while Daniel Niven was on stage. (His mother was on church committees with my father.) I met the guy on whose real-life exploits Steve McQueen's character in *The Great Escape* were based. (No, there was no dramatic motorcycle jump. In fact, he was still in "the cooler" after his last escape attempt when the big breakout happened. That was a good thing. Most of the POWs who did get out were rounded up and shot. All but three were recaptured. McQueen's role was a composite character based on a few different pilots who would escape and then deliberately get recaptured to be able to bring information on guard positions, railroad timetables, and other useful intelligence back to the men planning the escape.)

I no longer find it odd to see someone I know on the news. On the day I was writing this part of the introduction, a friend who is not a well-known newsmaker just showed up in a lead story in the *Wash-*

ington Post. My former hiking buddy and still friend was on the front page of the *Washington Post* the day "Don't Ask Don't Tell" ended as sort of the poster child for that cause. One day, as I listened to NPR in the car, I heard back-to-back-to-back stories covered by four NPR correspondents I know in four different places: Beth Accamando in San Diego, Jim Zarroli in New York, Kitte Felde in DC, and Jo Ann Allen in Denver. Another day, I heard two consecutive, completely unrelated news stories on NPR interviewing two people I knew from my neighborhood in Bethel Park, Pennsylvania: Dr. David Reitze and Dr. Christopher Newcomer. I used to cut their lawns.

I have been fortunate enough to have many opportunities to do things most people don't. I have worked in television, on music videos, and in other parts of show business, including doing standup comedy and MC-ing at the Friars Club in Beverly Hills. I taught traffic school to celebrities including Ben Stiller, Jackson Browne, and Marina Sirtis. I checked Josef Mengele's son into a motel. I've interviewed Alan Turing's nephew, and *Will & Grace* star Leslie Jordan.

I have had several of my screenplays optioned, but none made into movies. Yet. I have driven across the United States several times and, as of this writing, have been in 43 states and 10 countries. I have gotten to fly an open-cockpit biplane and ride a Zamboni, and I've met royalty.

Astute readers of this first chapter may have noticed that there is no mention of my birth or *David Copperfield*. I just wanted to get your attention and prepare you for a few other obscure references that may follow. And this is only "chapter" in the book. The rest of *If You Weren't Here…* is divided into sections. But most of the stories stand alone and you can jump in and read a random story from any part.

My adventures may not have made me rich or famous, but they have never left me bored. Welcome to some of those stories.

Table of Contents

IV. Brushes with Greatness

V. True Tales from Traffic School

VI. Writing Adventures

VII. The Coming Out Ring

To Book or Not to Book . . .
That is the Question

AFTER moving to Los Angeles, I got a job working at a branch of a popular chain bookstore. It was a very busy evening with just a few shopping days left before Christmas. The store was packed. Everyone was in a hurry and not in a very good mood. People were pushing their way to the register to demand things like, "Where is the new Danielle Steel book?" and one of the clerks, frantically ringing purchases at the register, would snap back, "Side wall. Under S." People in line were jostling others, trying to pay and get out. Many were complaining that we were out of something or didn't offer free gift-wrapping services.

In the midst of the noise and confusion, the phone rang. Ted, one of the many out-of-work actors who worked at the store, answered it, and yelled out across the crowded store, "Katherine!" Ted knew the store manager, Katherine, was somewhere in the store hidden by the mob of shoppers and shelves of books. For emphasis, and just to be goofy (as Ted was), he added, "But I shall call ye Kate for dainties are all Kates."

From out in the store, Katherine responded, "In good time! Let him that moved you hither, remove you hence. I know you at the first you were a moveable."

While still ringing up purchases, I yelled out, "Why, what's a moveable?"

Katherine replied, "A join'd stool."

A man in line said, "Thou hast hit it. Come sit on me."

Without missing a beat, a woman in the checkout line responded, "Asses are made to bear, and so are you."

About four guys in line now answered, "Women are made to bear, and so are you."

About six women replied, "No such jade as you, if me you mean."

Other people in line were puzzled by what was going on as ten men said, "Alas! good Kate, I will not burden thee; For, knowing thee to be but young and light…"

Even more women answered, " Too light for such a swain as you to catch; and yet as heavy as my weight should be."

Now when people got their purchases, instead of rushing off, they stuck around to continue playing their parts. Those who didn't know

Richard Burton as Mark Antony, front row, center, in a mural of movie stars in Hollywood.

what was going on stayed to see if there was some explanation for this madness. As more customers came in, they'd look around, confused; some would join in and others would stand there dumbfounded.

I heard a woman ask a man, "What's going on?"

He said, "We're doing Shakespeare. *Taming of the Shrew.*"

"Why?"

"I don't know." But he dutifully said Petruchio's next line. "What, with my tongue in your tail? Nay, come again, Good Kate; I am a gentleman."

Only in L.A. would dozens of out-of-work actors happen to have *Taming of the Shrew* memorized. I had recently played Petruchio in an acting class at Santa Monica College so still knew the part. I'm sure I couldn't keep up now.

I heard a customer ask, "What play is this?"

Another customer answered, "*Taming of the Shrew.* We're in Act II, Scene I... 'No cock of mine; you crow too like a craven.'"

Several people rushed to the bookstore's classics section and pulled down copies of the play. Once that idea spread, almost everyone who didn't know the play followed their lead, grabbed books and soon each line was read or said by thirty or forty people.

I heard someone ask, "Is this like Candid Camera? What's going on?"

The man just shrugged and said his line: "Now, by Saint George, I am too young for you."

The mood in the store had completely shifted. Now instead of being angry and impatient, people were lingering to see how this played out. Everyone was smiling. So as not to ruin the scene, instead of yelling, they were whispering, "I was looking for Jean Auel's new book..."

And the clerk would softly answer back where to find it.

No one was leaving the store and it was getting more crowded. At one point, I noticed a line at the payphone outside the store. This was pre-cell phone and I assumed people were calling friends to come down to the store, because the store was soon violating the fire code for occupancy.

A man quietly asked me, "I can't find any more copies of *Taming of the Shrew* in classics. Do you have more copies somewhere?"

I whispered, "I doubt it. We may have some in the back. But I don't have time to look, sorry. Maybe someone will share."

And a woman held out her copy and they shared. I wondered how many new friendships and relationships came out of this remarkable night.

"Go, fool, and whom thou keep'st command."

Taming of the Shrew goes on for about two hours from where we started, and instead of the enthusiasm for this project waning, the volume and number of participants kept growing.

"Fiddler, forbear; you grow too forward, sir: Have you so soon forgot the entertainment. Her sister Katharina welcomed you withal?"

People were still selecting books and all of us at the registers were still feverishly ringing up purchases.

"She says you have some goodly jest in hand: she will not come: she bids you come to her."

When we finally all said, "'Tis a wonder, by your leave, she will be tamed so," we gave ourselves a thunderous applause that must have lasted ten minutes.

Then there was a long happy afterglow of an evening well-spent and still no one moved to leave the now-packed store. Somewhere in the middle of the store, out of the silence came a voice. Katherine's voice. "What did you want, Ted?"

"Oh. There's a phone call for you."

Now we all burst out laughing knowing someone had been on hold for two hours. And of course anyone else trying to get through to the bookstore would have gotten a busy signal.

But that broke the special feeling that hung over the store and people started moving again, some leaving. People started talking to strangers.

"Hey, if we come back tomorrow night, could we do *Romeo and Juliet*?"

"I'd rather do a comedy. How about *As You Like It*?"

"*Twelfth Night* seems more appropriate for this time of year."

The suggestions kept coming with nothing decided by the time most of the participants had left and it was time to close the store. When we totaled up sales, it was one of our largest nights ever, all without missing a beat in the play.

We wondered if anyone would actually show up the following evening to continue this, but if anyone did come for Shakespeare, they didn't say anything and the crowd in the store didn't seem larger than normal for Christmas. I and the rest of the staff were a little disappointed. I guess we all knew there was no way to recreate the spontaneity and magic of that night.

For a week we found stray copies of the play all over the bookstore. We sold a few copies that night, but most were abandoned and only a few returned to their shelf, and many of those were creased and wrinkled and unsaleable.

It wasn't exactly *Shakespeare in the Park*, but it was a fabulous, unrehearsed, impromptu flash mob—before the term flash mob even existed. And alas, Petruchio, also before cell phones so there is no video of this marvelous event.

The Boy from Leeds-of-the-Valley

ONE of the bookstore clerks who was already working there when I started was Colin. Colin was adorable and had a beautiful English accent. He was about 20 years old and hailed from Leeds, England. He was as charming and welcoming as a warm spot o' tea on a cold British morning. Everyone loved Colin.

One day I was working the register when a man came in and asked if Colin was around. I said, yes, he was in the backroom. I asked one of the other clerks to go fetch him. The man said he was Colin's father and that Colin had forgotten his lunch. The father said he happened to be in the area and thought he'd drop it off since in all the months Colin had worked there, he had never seen the store. I said that was nice of him and added, "So, I guess your wife must be British."

He said, "No, why would you think that?"

"Well, because you're not and your son is."

He looked startled and said, "My son is *what*?"

At that moment Colin appeared from the back room and even from 30 feet away we could hear him swallow hard. He cleared his throat a few times and said uh and um and ah a few times and it was apparent why he was hesitating to speak. He didn't know what accent to use. His father's unexpected appearance at the store had blown his cover and his jig was up. The whole story came out. Colin decide that being born and raised in "The Valley"—the San Fernando Valley—was, well, boring. So when he started high school, he reinvented himself as a kid who had just moved from Leeds. He had done extensive research on Leeds. What street he lived on, what football team he'd have rooted for, the school he went to. He even learned to do a Leeds accent.

Apparently Leeds has a distinct accent and I recalled Brits shopping in the bookstore recognizing it and commenting on it. I remember one conversation a few weeks earlier when an Englishman picked up on the accent and struck up a conversation with Colin. Colin knew everything the man mentioned: of course he remembered that park, he used to play there as a child, and oh, yes, didn't that tea shop have the best biscuits? Colin missed them so much!

I still marvel at the amount of homework he must have done to have memorized his fake hometown. And, in those pre-internet days, how did he manage to nail the accent? Now I am sure he could google a tutorial, but back then that level of commitment took work and ingenuity. Colin had left his home every day for high school in The Valley and transformed himself into the unique British student. He'd return home each afternoon as another boring Valley boy. His father, the other bookstore employees, and I were all stunned. Batman's mask had just been ripped off revealing a very ordinary Bruce Wayne. His father left telling Colin they would talk at home that evening. He clearly needed time to process what he had just learned.

The next day, everyone at the bookstore was still talking about it. Our boss (the manager) was equally dumbfounded when she heard the truth. She was still flabbergasted when our district manager happened in and our boss spilled out the bizarre story to her supervisor. The district manager was also shocked. Over the months Colin had worked there, he had brought her under his quaint British-boy spell as well. The district manager asked to see Colin's employee paperwork, curious about what it said about his past. She read it and then told our store manager to fire Colin. We were all upset. Why, we all asked. Because he had lied on his application. His paperwork was all fiction. Our store manager and our staff argued that Colin was a great employee. Never late. Hard worker. His cash register drawer was always correct. We all loved him. Customers loved him. He was good for business. We didn't want him fired. Please let him stay! But she was adamant, and I never saw Colin again. He was fired over the phone.

There was great irony in the district manager firing someone for lying. It was well known that she was having an affair with her boss, although they were both married to other people. She had also made it quite clear to me and the other cute young guys at work that she would be open to having a fling with any of us. When she later took maternity leave, we all speculated behind her back as to whose baby it might be.

Should I Call You Sir Richard?

THE bookstore where I worked in Beverly Hills was one block from Rodeo Drive so a host of celebrities shopped there. The Bridges family—Lloyd, Jeff, and Beau—used to come in together. Jane Fonda was still married to Tom Hayden and they would shop together. Fred Astaire came in often and would usually trip over something. He was quite elderly by then and we were worried he would get hurt and we'd make the news for the store having caused the most graceful man ever to have hurt himself. Cybil Shepherd shopped there at the height of her *Moonlighting* popularity. And Richard Burton would come in almost every day.

At the store, we had an unwritten policy that we'd never call anyone by name or do anything to draw attention to the stars, thinking they should be able to shop in their own neighborhood without being bothered.

Burton was then living in the penthouse of the Beverly Wilshire Hotel, about four blocks from the bookstore so it was convenient for him to walk over. He would buy a thick hardback book every visit. He seemed to read a massive book a day. I asked him about it once and he said he had nothing else to do. He seemed lonely and worn down by life. I had to look it up. He would have then been about 57 years old then but could easily have passed for 75.

Some days he would buy six or eight more copies of a book he had just bought a few days earlier. I asked him about that and he said, "At my age, almost everyone I know is in hospital or a nursing home, so if I find a good book, I buy extras and take a copy when I go visiting." He seemed a very thoughtful person. And certainly well-read. His tastes were James Michener, Sidney Sheldon, and some spy thrillers, as well as more esoteric selections.

Almost everyone else who worked there were aspiring actors and they would turn into babbling fools, awestruck by the presence of the great Sir Richard Burton. One of the wannabe actors who worked there, Daniel, who fresh off the turnip truck from Kansas, was particularly agog at seeing his hero. He would never want to wait on Burton or ring up his purchases, preferring to study the esteemed actor from afar. Daniel had shared his fantasy with the rest of the staff that he was going to think of something so brilliant to say to Burton that Burton would be so impressed he'd say, "Well, young man, I am doing a play in London next month, and you would be perfect to play my grandson!"

Until Daniel figured out what that perfect line was, he hid from Burton and stalked him around the store. Until that one day when Daniel was shelving books, his back to the door, when Burton came in. Burton put a hand on Daniel's shoulder and said, "So, young man, what looks good today."

As I and other employees watched, Daniel, his face now inches from his god, turned white and he stammered something like, "Bufdfd. Dfefe.

Fereddner. Sdfeenn. Smerfeddrd," too star-struck to form a real word, let alone an inspirational sentence. Burton took his hand off Daniel's shoulder, looked at it as though it might be diseased, wiped it off on his shirt, and walked away. (While those of us behind the cash registers laughed our asses off.) But now Daniel really had to hide when Burton came in because the noted thespian thought Daniel was an idiot. Daniel was too embarrassed to face him ever again. If Burton came in while Daniel was working a register, he'd ask someone else to cover for him and he'd go hide in the back room until after Burton left.

One day I was shelving books in the back of the store when Burton, who by this time often asked me for recommendations he might like, came up to me and said, in that melodious Welsh accent, "Walt, can I ask you something?" (We wore nametags and he always was polite enough to call us by name and remember our names.)

I said yes, assuming he wanted more book recommendations.

Instead he said, "Do you know who I am?"

I replied, "Of course, Mr. Burton. Uh, er, or should I call you Sir Richard?"

He laughed and said, "I don't really care what you call me. I just thought you don't know who I am. You don't act like it."

"Is that a problem?"

He said no. I was the only one in the store who didn't drool on his shoes or turn into a blithering idiot when I was talking to him, so he wondered if perhaps I wasn't a movie fan or just didn't know who he was. He said he liked that we could just have normal conversations about books without the fawning.

I told him about our informal policy not to call stars by name to give them a little privacy, so I never addressed him by name. I told him I loved his work, especially *Virginia Woolf*. And I told him I felt a little kinship with him because my great-grandmother was born in Wales, not far from where he was from. After that, I was like his long-lost relative and he treated me with even more bonhomie. We had many more interesting conversations. Then he moved to Switzerland, where he died not long after.

Playing the Piano. Badly.

WHEN my store manager was offered a store much closer to her home in Glendale, she asked me to go with her and be assistant manager there.

It often happened that we would interact via phone with the stores closest to us. If we were out of a book, a customer might ask us to call nearby branch stores to see if they had it. If we ran out of bags or credit card slips or they did, we'd arrange to borrow among the locations. We got friendly with the folks at the nearest store and would sometimes even meet them for a drink after work. Our acquaintance with them made their actions more shocking. In early January, the district manager for that area showed up at our store with wild news.

The manager and both assistant managers of the other store had been fired and were going to be prosecuted unless they made restitution in 60 days.

In mid-December, they launched a bold plan. They would "borrow" $20,000 from the bookstore. In the pre-Christmas shopping rush, most stores would take in more than $10,000 a day in cash. We had three days after close of business to deposit the credit card slips and cash. Their plan was to borrow enough cash to buy a large amount of marijuana from one of the employee's dealer's dealer. They were going up a couple of notches on the supply chain to make a big buy. Purchase in quantity to get the bulk discount. Then they'd break down the pounds into ounces, quarter ounces, and other smaller amounts to resell it. They already had customers lined up to buy enough to cover the initial "loan" fast then they'd have time to sell the rest and that would all be profit. A lot of profit. They were looking to make $100,000 on the bookstore's $20,000 investment.

One slight problem. The big-time dealer wasn't keen on the competition in his neighborhood. He stole their $20,000. They were rank amateurs going up against a seasoned pro. And if your drug connection rips you off, you can't really call the cops and complain, now can you?

Until Christmas, they were able to cover the previous day's receipts, always staying two days behind in deposits. After Christmas, the store's daily cash intake was $3000 at most. They would now have to save up several days' cash to make one deposit and were getting further and further behind. Upper management noticed. Shockingly, they didn't call the police. The bookstore chain just wanted its money back and after firing the three thieves was giving them two months to come up with the cash. I never heard the outcome, if they ever did find a way to pay off their debt or if they were prosecuted.

I liked the quaint phrase the district manager used to describe their theft. He was from Colombia, and apparently an idiom they use down there refers to stealing from the till as "playing the piano" as in "having talented fingers." That crew from the other store couldn't even play *Chopsticks* without getting caught.

II. Shit Like This Only Happens When You're Around

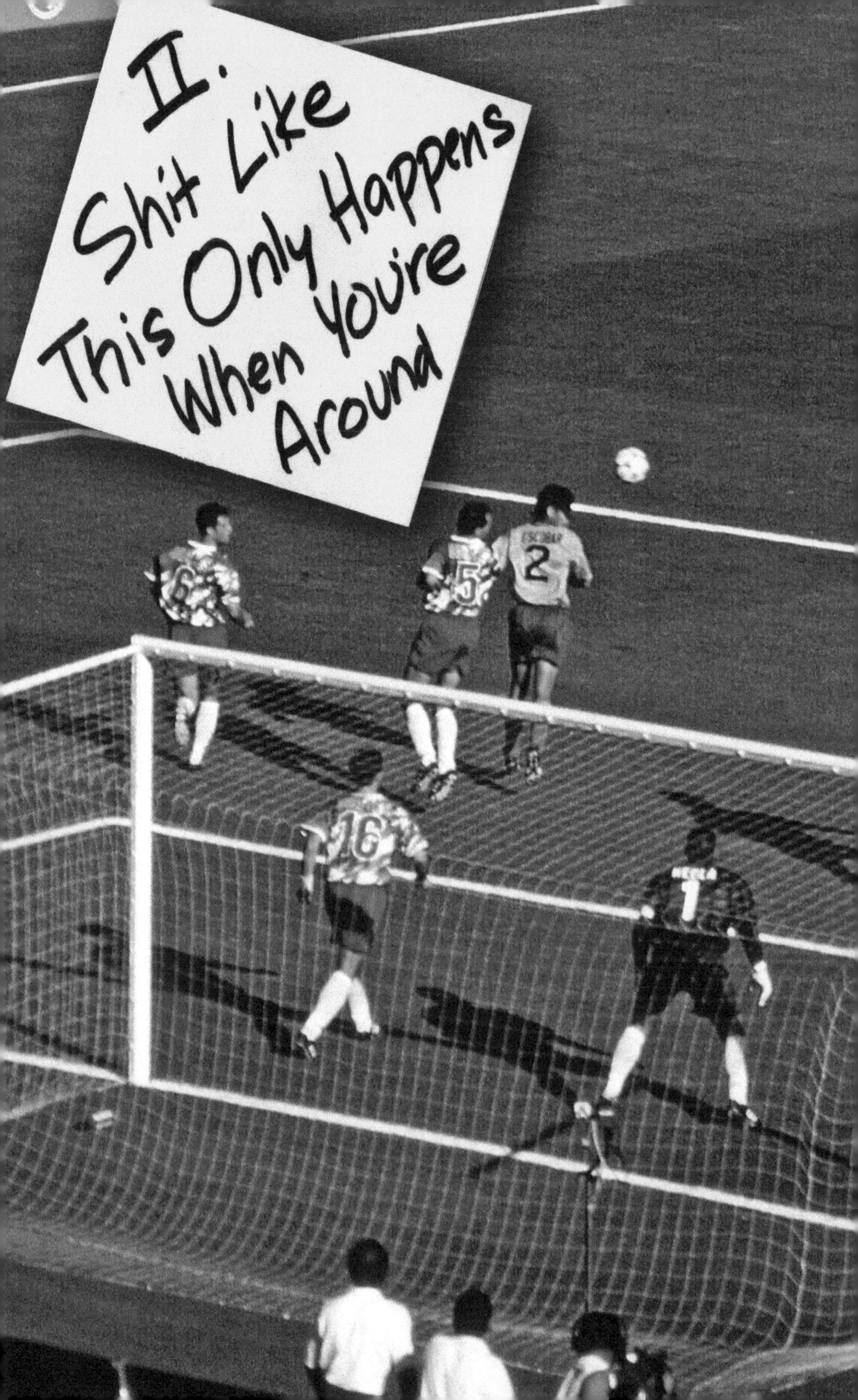

Sometimes It's Better Not to Ask

ONE night I arrived home at my apartment in Venice, California about 10:00 p.m. after teaching a traffic school class. As I drove down the alley and pulled into the parking place under the building, I was surprised to see an LAPD car parked across the alley in front of my neighbors' house. Two officers were talking to Mr. and Mrs. Linden.

As I got out of my car, one of the cops approached me. He asked, "Excuse me, do you live here?"

I started to answer and he interrupted, saying, "First, let me explain you're not suspected of anything. Nor are you under arrest and you can refuse to answer any of my questions and just walk away. But I'd like to ask you to help out your police department this evening if you're willing."

I said I was and that I lived in the apartment above the carport where we were standing.

He said, "Just the way things are going this evening, would you mind if I asked for some ID so I know who I'm dealing with. Again, you can refuse."

Knowing I hadn't done anything for which I could possibly be wanted, I pulled out my wallet and when I went to pull out my driver's license, my paper traffic school instructor's license sort of stuck to the back of my driver's license and fell out on the concrete. The cop picked it up and looked at it.

He said, "You teach traffic school?" I said I did. He said, "They do a pretty good background check for that don't they? So you're not crazy?"

Startled, I asked, "What kind of a question is that?"

And he pointed to the trio across the street and said, "See the people standing with my partner over there? Are they crazy?"

"What!? You mean Judge Linden and his wife?"

The cop hung his head. "Shit. You mean he really is a judge?"

"You didn't call them crazy, did you?"

"Yeah, I kinda did."

"Why would you do that? He's a judge of the Superior Court. His wife is one of the top Republican committee people in the state. She claims huge credit for getting George Deukmejian elected governor."

"Shit," the cop said again.

Escobar, (in the yellow #2 jersey for Colombia), in their famous match against the U.S. in the 1994 World Cup preliminaries at the Rose Bowl.

"Shit is right. Why would you call them crazy?"

"Because they called the police about a crazy story about a guy in a jockstrap with a paper heart climbing over the house next to theirs. When we came out to check it out, they told us the woman next door wouldn't come to the door at night because she didn't have electricity or running water. Then they started telling us about four tons of garbage. And a dead body in the backyard and..."

"Oh, that's all true!"

"Huh?"

"Well I don't know anything about the guy in the jockstrap, but the rest is true. There was four tons of garbage in that lady's house. And they found a body in the backyard."

The cop looked at me carefully thinking I might also be crazy. But he said, "Since they know you, would you be willing to come across the street with me and help sort this out and smooth things over a bit?"

I said sure. I was intrigued and always up for a good story. And the Lindens were nice people. I walked over and said good evening to them. They said hello to me through clenched teeth. They were both clearly seething at the cops.

The cop to whom I had been speaking pointed to me and told his partner, "This guy lives across the street and he said he knows the woman next door doesn't have electricity and won't open her door after dark. The partner nodded, but was still slightly confused.

Judge Linden was furious and yelled at the cops, "You'll believe him, but you won't believe me?"

I asked the judge, "Didn't you tell him who you were?"

"I did! They didn't believe me!"

The cops looked sheepish.

I asked, "Don't you have an ID or something that says that you're a judge?"

"I do, but they wouldn't let me out of their sight to go inside and get it!"

"What's going on with the crazy lady?" I asked. All of the neighbors referred to the woman with no electricity as *the crazy lady*. She was. More on that soon.

Mrs. Linden said, "I looked out the upstairs window and saw a man in nothing but a jockstrap climbing over the roof of the house next door. I called for Gene (her husband) to come and look. The man saw us and started climbing down from the roof. That's when we noticed he had a red paper heart pinned to the front of the jockstrap, covering his, uh…well…I said I'd call 9-1-1 while Gene went down to try to see where the man went or what he was up to."

Gene Linden picked up the story. "I followed him, at a distance, and he went into that house down there," he said, pointing about a block down the alley. "I wanted these officers to check it out, but…" He leveled a scathing look at the two cops. "Now will you walk down there with me?"

Having not much choice, the five of us walked down the alley — the two Lindens, the two cops, and me. We got to the house which Judge Linden said he had seen the man in the jockstrap enter. There were lights on in the house and someone was moving behind the curtains.

One of the cops went up on the porch while the other cop stood with the rest of us in the alley, a few feet away. The cop rang the doorbell. Someone peeked out the door. The lights in the house went out. The cop looked down from the porch at us, exasperated.

The cop rang the doorbell again and loudly announced, "This is the Los Angeles Police Department, please open the door!" We could see and hear scurrying inside the house. The cop who clearly was already frustrated after this odd evening yelled, "Look. We know you're in there. We can see and hear you. Right now we just want to ask you a few questions." More scurrying. "Don't think you can go out the back. My partner is out back."

We all looked at the other cop in the alley with us who sort of shrugged and took a couple of steps back so he was not in the line of sight from the windows.

The cop on the porch knocked again. "Don't play games. We know you're in there. Open the door and answer a few questions and we'll be fine. If not, we have a witness to a probable crime; we can get a warrant and wait here until it arrives. If it comes to that, I can pretty much guarantee you, someone is getting arrested. So open the door!"

There was more scurrying. Then the door slowly opened. Standing in the doorway was a man, probably about 40 years old, naked except for a jockstrap with a red paper heart pinned over the front pouch.

Judge Linden said, "See? I told you! How would I know he was wearing that if he hadn't been climbing around the crazy lady's house?"

The man in the doorway indignantly replied to Judge Linden, "You were probably peeking in my windows again!"

A now furious judge yelled, "I was not peeking in your windows! You were crawling around on the roof of that house!"

The cop said to the jock-strapped man, "It's pretty clear you were out this evening. What's going on?"

The man hesitated and tried to evade a little, but the cop kept pressing him, reinforced now and then with the threat of arrest and going to jail dressed like that. Finally, the man said, "Okay. I was out for a minute. My cat got out." He reached down and picked up a shaggy, fat cat as proof. "She's an indoor cat so I was afraid of what would happen if she got out. I chased her down the alley. She climbed up on the roof of the crazy lady's house. I knocked on the crazy lady's door, but of course she didn't answer. My cat hates heights and was sort of panicking up there so I climbed up to get her down."

After a few more questions, the cops and the Lindens seemed satisfied with the guy's explanation and we walked back down the alley. On the way, I asked the cop why he didn't ask about the guy's unusual outfit and he replied, "The way tonight is going, he probably would have told me and I wasn't sure I wanted to hear whatever that explanation might be. Sometimes it's best not to know."

The "Crazy Lady" of Venice

WHEN I first moved into the apartment on Pacific Avenue in Venice, I had noticed the elderly woman who lived across the alley, a couple of doors down. Her home faced the Grand Canal out the other side.

One night she was pushing her car from one side of the alley to the other for street sweeping day. I helped her push the car. She was not very friendly and not at all grateful. I didn't ask why she was pushing it instead of starting it and driving it in a U-turn to re-park it as everyone else did to avoid a ticket on certain days. I had also seen her filling up buckets of water at the hose tap under our building in the parking area. I guess I should have wondered why.

A neighbor saw me helping her push the car again a few weeks later and said that everyone else had gotten over doing that. She did it every week and she could easily drive it. She just didn't want to use the gas to drive it 60 feet. This struck me as odd, but I did stop helping her push the car.

I learned from the neighbors that she didn't have electricity or running water. She took water from neighbors' hose taps for her home use. She locked up after dark and didn't use any lights of any kind. Not even candles. She would not open the door for any reason at night. I felt sorry for her, thinking she was so poor, but the other neighbors said she wasn't penniless, just crazy.

The neighborhood was going to find out just how mentally ill she was. One morning I went out to get in my car to go teach traffic school and I saw an odd conglomeration of vehicles in the alley. There were two LAPD patrol cars. Two firetrucks. A skip loader, a backhoe, and several large dump trucks. Working around these vehicles were several

Earth-moving equipment and city trucks attending to the mess in the elderly woman's house under the mural that says, "Beautify Venice."

firefighters, police officers, and what appeared to be city road workers in hard hats. The action was centered around the Crazy Lady's house, but I had to get to work and didn't have time to investigate. I came home nine hours later, and the crew was still there carrying shovelfuls of junk. They worked until 9 or 10 at night with one fire truck and crew remaining overnight. Work resumed early the next morning. But I went off to my job.

Day three, the work continued. I was more than curious so I went up to the guy in a hard hat with the metal clipboard with a lid on it. That kind of clipboard is always a sign of authority on a job site. He said he was indeed in charge. I asked what was going on. He seemed surprised that I didn't know as though word had already spread through the neighborhood. I told him I had not been home much or seen any of the neighbors to ask.

He said that a few days earlier the mailman had noticed the woman had not taken her mail out of the box for several days. He knew she never went anywhere, so he wondered if something was wrong. Letter carriers often end up being the first ones to notice something is amiss. The mailman knocked on the door and got no reply so he looked in the window. Inside he saw a mountain of garbage had avalanched and sticking up out of it appeared to be a hand.

He went to a neighbor's house and asked them to call 9-1-1. The police and a fire unit responded. They radioed for back-up, and it took several crews several hours to dig her out. She had been buried for days and was dehydrated and very weak. They took her to the hospital where she was recovering.

Meanwhile the firefighters had called the department of the guy with the clipboard to whom I was speaking. His department specializes in cases like this and got an emergency court order to start cleaning out her house as a fire and health hazard.

He said they had been digging for days and only cleared the garage and living room. He said there were stacks of newspapers and magazines from floor to ceiling. The ones at the bottom were dated 1948, over 40 years earlier. Like an archeological dig, they were using the base level to determine when this started. There was one narrow walkway through the living room to the kitchen to the bedroom. Every place else was stacked with garbage, mostly sorted by type. For instance, he said there was an entire bedroom full of empty cat food cans. And she didn't own a cat, so apparently this is what she had been eating. He said the stacks of papers in the slot canyon through the living room had collapsed on the unfortunate woman and she was buried alive. Lucky for her, the mailman was vigilant, or she would have only lasted another day or two.

I was flabbergasted by what he was telling me. He offered to let me take a peek inside and I said, "No, I'm good. I can smell it from here." I remember she'd had a second story put on the house at one point while I was living there. Apparently its only purpose was to store more trash.

He said it would take at least another two weeks to empty and fumigate the house.

I said that clearly it needed to be done, but I was curious as to who paid for all of this. This was a lot of manpower tied up and a lot of overtime. A fire crew standing by in case the papers flared up. A pair of cops on site 24 hours a day to watch the house since the front door and window had been removed.

He said, "She will."

I said, "What makes you think she has money to pay for all of this? She steals water from our hose faucet."

He said, "We'll bill her. And if she doesn't pay, we'll take out a lien against this house or one of her other properties."

I looked quizzically at him. He went on to explain, "She has properties worth tens of millions of dollars. She owns a whole block in Westwood [the very expensive neighborhood where UCLA is located], she owns several blocks in the San Fernando Valley including huge apartment buildings and shopping centers."

He could tell I was very confused. I started to argue, "But she…"

He shook his head. "We go through this all the time. She is clearly mentally ill. We always investigate these cases to see what we're up against. She is, or I guess I should say was, a countess. From Hungary, I think. She lost her family and everything they had—their home, all their possessions, everything in the Second World War. After the war, she made her way to L.A., where she met and married a budding real estate mogul who was buying up land while it was cheap. He just really got things going when, a couple years into their marriage, he died. She had valuable property and this house, but nothing and no one else."

I was stunned by what I was hearing.

He went on to say the City of Los Angeles had about ten of these cases a year. And often it involved someone who had suffered some catastrophic loss and so they started hoarding thing to compensate. Don't throw that newspaper or magazine out, you may need it someday. He said their purchases made no rational sense. They wouldn't spend money on running water, but they'd put on a second story to store more empty cat food cans. They were beyond being rational; they were mentally ill.

He pointed out a new silver Mercedes parked a few hundred feet away. I hadn't noticed the man in the car that had been there every day. My attention was drawn to the much bigger vehicles all around. Mr. Clipboard said the man in the car was the woman's attorney. He was counting the number of shovelfuls of stuff they were removing because she intended to sue the city for stealing her property. He said this was also quite typical. She saw the garbage as having great value, but they always got the court cases against the city dismissed—after all, what is the street value of a 20-year-old empty cat food can? But she was going to pay that lawyer a few hundred dollars an hour to do what she requested. The lawyer knew it was a fool's errand and every day he visited the woman in the hospital and asked her to reconsider. Every day she asked him why he wasn't keeping watch over her property like she was paying him to do.

It took about two weeks for the crews to finish cleaning out the house as dump truck after dump truck hauled away this woman's "treasures." Now that I knew the story, it made me very sad. I didn't want the mess to stay—after a few days, I could smell the stench coming from the house all the way across the alley. I heard clipboard guy's stories of the rats and roaches. It truly was a health and safety hazard.

But I could only imagine that mentally ill woman coming home to her empty house. Imagine coming home from vacation and finding your house empty. Every possession gone. From what Mr. Clipboard said, in her mind there was no difference between her "valuables" and my TV and computer and keepsakes.

Ironically, above her garage was a lovely little bit of art that said, "Beautify Venice, the Dream That Made a City." There was a drawing of an Italian-style gondolier poling his gondola and underneath is said, "Venice by the Sea".

A few months later, I saw police and a black van, the kind the coroner's office uses, at the woman's home. I wondered if she had died. I went down to the alley to see what was going on. A few neighbors were already out there. The woman's next-door neighbor, Mrs. Linden, who later had to deal with the guy with the jock and the paper heart, was there. I asked her if she knew what was going on.

She said that the garbage collectors came by every week and were smelling a different stench than the usual one coming from the house, which had not been nearly as bad after the cleanup but was still lingering. Each week the odor got worse and ranker. One of the garbage men finally decided to hoist himself up her fence to see what was causing it. There, in the countess's backyard, was a decomposing body.

Mrs. Linden went on to say that the woman had somehow acquired a gentleman caller who would come over to visit her. One night after the elderly couple had eaten dinner, he took the trash out and never came back. The woman assumed he had just left her. She may have been wealthy, but she was severely mentally ill, and I can't imagine trying to eat in a house that had no electricity or running water and a smell that would make a maggot vomit. So maybe she understood why he left.

He *had* left. This mortal coil. Since she never took out any trash— she had already started accumulating stuff again—she never went in the backyard to know his body had been lying there for weeks. Apparently the old man had a heart attack on the way to the trash can. And the smell inside the house was so bad she hadn't noticed what even the garbage collectors had.

I moved from Venice in 1992, so don't know what happened to her or if the house continued to refill the trash or if the city kept tabs on that or tried to get her mental health counseling. I hope her fate was better than that of her date.

The Fanny Pack Bandit

M Y cell phone rang. I didn't recognize the number, but I answered it. It was my old roommate from my Venice days, Ron. I hadn't heard from him in years. He asked if I had heard from our other roommate from those days, Dave.

I told Ron I had not heard him in years, why would I have heard from Dave? He said he just got a call from Dave, after years of hearing nothing. It was Dave's one phone call from the federal holding facility in San Bernardino. Dave was in federal custody. "For what?" I asked. Ron said he didn't know. Ron's cell phone dropped the call before Dave could say much. He waited for Dave to call back, but apparently when they say you get one phone call, you get one call whether the call stays connected or not. Ron wondered if I knew what was going on. I told him I did not. I hadn't heard from him or Dave in years, so I had no idea. I added that I was in the middle of being trained on a new job and really didn't have time to discuss it right now, could he call me back that evening?

When Ron called me a few hours later, he had done some research. It seemed our erstwhile roommate was the "Fanny Pack Bandit." He had robbed 13 banks in the Los Angeles area! He would stick the money in a fanny pack and walk briskly from the bank, so law enforcement had given him that cute moniker.

He was captured in a way that was so typically Dave. He robbed a bank in the Brentwood section of Los Angeles, and was calmly, but swiftly, walking away from the scene of the crime when the dye pack exploded in his fanny pack, covering his midsection in pink. Several FBI agents were having lunch on the outdoor patio of the Souplantation next to the bank. They saw the puff of pink, stood up, drew their weapons, and ordered Dave to stop. Thus ended the career of the Fanny Pack Bandit. Ron and I found this rather sad, fitting, and funny.

We were both puzzled as to why Dave wasted his one phone call on Ron, because as Ron said, "There was no way I was going to drive to San Bernardino to bail him out! Why would he call me after all these years?"

A little bit of the sad backstory of Dave. He was a super nice guy. Sweet smile and just enough of a southern accent to be charming. He was also an addict. Ron and I knew he drank too much. We saw the empties and knew he disposed of a lot of bottles thinking we didn't see them. Both of us had opened the front door more than once to find him passed out on the exterior steps of the building. His last effort somehow got him home, but climbing the 20 or so stairs was too much for him. Some days his keys would be in the front door and he'd be face down in front of the door as though just putting the key in the lock was his final movement before dying. Neighbors could hardly fail to notice this behavior and remark on it.

His other problem came to our attention when the downstairs neighbors had a plumbing issue. Water was seeping through the ceiling in their bathroom, which clearly meant it was coming from the pipes in the bathroom above. The landlady asked if I would be home on a certain day and could let the plumber in to take a look. I showed the plumber Dave's bathroom. I waited in the living room, just outside Dave's bedroom in case the plumber needed me for anything, but not wanting to crowd the man while he worked.

When I heard him exclaim, "Holy fucking shit!" I ran into the bedroom and to the bathroom door, asking as I went, "Is the plumbing problem that bad?"

He moved aside to show me what was in the vanity cabinet under the sink and said, "No, the drug problem is that bad."

Behind the row of cleaning products that most people have under their sinks were vials. Dozens, if not hundreds of little glass vials, each containing a rock of crack cocaine. The entire vanity was full to a depth of about 18 inches of them. Enough to fill your average picnic cooler. I assured the plumber I was unaware of this stash, and that I'd deal with it.

That night when Ron got home, I discussed it with him, and we agreed Dave had to go. We were barely able to tolerate the drinking. The drugs, and the risk that posed to us if the police heard about the large cache of crack, was too much. We had a polite talk with Dave and asked him to move out. He understood.

Apparently, years later he had chosen to support his habit by robbing banks. And apparently he was successful at it for a while.

I eventually did hear from Dave after he got out of prison. He was oddly angry about

some of what seemed to me to be the wrong aspects of his arrest and incarceration. One of the first things he told me was that he hated that the press had referred to him as the "Fanny Pack Bandit." It thought it made him sound weak. He wanted a tough nickname.

He also was not happy at the way he got caught. He said, "I specifically told that bitch [*the bank teller*] NO DYE PACK! And what did she do??" Seriously, what is the world coming to when you can't even trust the bank teller you're robbing!? Next, he learned in prison (whether this is true, I don't know) that the FBI's rules say they are not allowed to shoot you in the back unless you are wanted for murder, or presenting a clear danger to others. He said, "I'm still pretty fast. I could've run for it. They'd have had to jump the fence and the hedge at Souplantation. I had my escape route planned out. I'd have zigged down a side street, down the alley, and if I could just lose them. I'd have had a pretty good head start and I don't think they'd have caught up. I wish I had known they weren't allowed to just shoot me."

He was also misinformed about what would happen to him, and where he'd end up. He said he had done research and that as long as you didn't really have a gun, they couldn't charge you with armed robbery so at worst, if he got caught, he would get charged with a lesser crime. Apparently, if you feign a gun as he had and terrorized a bank teller, it counts as armed robbery. (I don't know for a fact that this is true, either, but so he told me.) He had researched which crime to commit so if he got caught, he'd find himself in a federal pen rather than a state prison, which were rumored to be more dangerous, had worse food, and generally weren't as nice. I had never thought to shop for which sort of prison I might want to go to before deciding what law to break.

He was sure that because it wasn't a violent crime if he didn't have a gun, and hadn't hurt anyone, he'd get a light sentence and he'd get sent to one of the famous "Club Feds." Since he was in SoCal, he was certain that it would be the one on the beach near Lompoc. He didn't know that by then the "Club Feds" were a thing of the past, and that they could send you wherever they damn well pleased.

He ended up doing three years, which struck me as not very severe given the number of robberies, but maybe he pleaded guilty to save them a trial. He got sent to a prison camp in Louisiana. A place with no air conditioning. In a sweaty swamp in Louisiana. A far cry from beach volleyball in Lompoc!

When he got out, he returned to L.A. and reached out to me for a job reference. That didn't happen. He still calls me every few months. I always seem to be too busy to talk. He has told me that he still considers Ron and I his closest friends, even though we threw him out of the apartment. I feel bad for him, but I don't need that much dangerous crazy in my life.

America Doesn't Have Talent

A MONG my talents, I would not count singing as one. Although I enjoy music, I can't play it, I can't sing, and I can't dance. I am pretty much tone-deaf with no sense of rhythm. But I do enjoy listening and am glad I took clarinet and drum lessons as a child. Although I was terrible at both, I did learn to read music. In college, I took a class in classical musical appreciation which broadened my tastes and my appreciation of music immensely.

I tend to avoid karaoke nights because almost inevitably people will try to goad me into singing. An embarrassment I don't need—and damage to their ears they don't need. I also am not a big fan of karaoke because of the other bad singing one often has to endure at those events.

I used to belong to a writers' group that met in Long Beach and even after I moved to San Diego, I continued to drive up once a month for their meetings. I would stay over at a friend's the night before the meeting and spend the day either in meetings in L.A. or lunching with friends, or, if nothing else, writing on my laptop in a coffee shop. The night before our meeting was karaoke night at the Silver Fox Bar in Long Beach, two blocks from my friend's condo.

I would walk over to the Fox, sometimes with my friend and we would enjoy the karaoke performances; we knew we would never be asked to sing. From the caliber of the performers, I think you had to have been in at least six Broadway musicals and have a Grammy on your resume to qualify to be on that stage. It almost seemed you had to audition to get a time slot.

They did not want amateurs or people who couldn't carry a tune. If someone who didn't have golden pipes had the temerity to take the mic, they would be summarily judged by a jury of their more musical peers and be driven from the stage by a chorus of boos that grew louder until the offending party had no choice but to retreat. Tough crowd.

The flip side of that is they were appreciative of those who could sing well. And some of the singers who were there every Wednesday clearly rehearsed because their performances were worthy of a record deal. Some must have rehearsed with other singers because they rocked four-part harmonies that were amazing; others performed Motown hits complete with a backing chorus Gladys Knight would want to hire.

One week, I found myself in Long Beach a day early, so I went to the Silver Fox for a beer and hopes of some entertainment. Tuesday night it seemed was piano bar karaoke. The place was far less crowded than the standing-room-only mob for Wednesday's songfest. There was a seat open around the piano and everyone else in the bar was there and when I was beckoned over, I joined them.

The few people who sang before me were decent. Not bad, but nowhere near the talent I was used to at the Fox. The guy next to me finished singing and passed me the mic. I passed it to the person next to me. The piano player who had been diddling the keys between each performance stopped playing and looked at me. "No. No, no, no. If you are going to sit at my piano, you have to sing."

I said, "I'm sorry, but no. No one wants to hear me sing. Not even me in the shower."

He said, "Everybody has to sing."

"I can't sing."

Others around the piano joined in trying to encourage me to participate, saying, "Everybody can sing," or "Everybody has at least one song they can do. Pick something."

I should note that I am so bad that even though everyone in my class was supposed to be part of the chorus for my eighth grade graduation, the teacher asked me just to lip sync and fake it because when I actually sang, I was so off-key I threw off the people around me.

I said to the assembled patrons around the piano, "Let me put it this way. I am so bad that if I were to yell fire into this microphone this bar wouldn't clear out as rapidly as it would if I start singing."

They insisted. Clearly the evening was at a standstill until I sang something. After much cajoling, I settled on Billy Joel's *Piano Man*, a song I know well. (Apologies to Billy Joel for how I was about to mangle it.) The pianist started playing and at the appropriate moment, I started singing. I got out about four words before he lunged across the piano and yanked the microphone from my hand. He said, "Please, please, do not ever do that in public again."

I said, "I told you so. The next time someone says they can't sing, believe them."

A few years later a friend and I went to a party on Christmas in northern San Diego County. When the party broke up, we weren't quite ready to go home so we stopped in at a bar in Oceanside. It being Christmas night, there were only about 10 people in the bar. And it was karaoke night. As usual, the other patrons wanted us to join the queue to sing. We both declined. My friend said, "No one wants to hear me sing. I am terrible."

I said, "I'm sure I'm worse."

One thing led to another and the other patrons teased us into a sing-off. The reward was the loser—the worse singer—got a free drink. The winner—the less bad of the two of us—got free drinks the rest of the night. Given the congenial atmosphere and the premise of an *America Doesn't Have Any Talent* contest, we agreed.

At least I can now say, 1) I have finished a full song at a karaoke night and 2) I am NOT the worst singer in the world.

A Random Act of Kindness

FOR a website called *The Real Us*, I was asked to write about performing a random act of kindness. This is the story I shared.

It was my first winter in California after graduating from Penn State. One afternoon, as I walked by a thrift shop, I was surprised to see two Penn State mugs in their window.

The little mugs were cute. They appeared to be handmade ceramics with a funny face capped by a mortar board, complete with tassel, and had the name of my alma mater etched above the eyebrows. I went into the shop and was surprised by how cheap they were—fifty cents each! I took both up to the cash register.

The clerk had taken my money, while an elderly woman was speaking to another clerk at the next register. The lady was saying that she only had a dollar, but the winter jacket was six dollars, and she wondered if she could put a dollar down and make payments as she got the money. She said she would really need the jacket as winter was coming, but...

*The cute ceramic
Penn State mug.*

The clerk explained that they did not have a layaway plan and that they could hold it for a day, no more. The lady said she wouldn't have the rest of the money by the next day.

I motioned my clerk toward me and leaned toward her. I held out a five-dollar bill and said, "I'd like to pay for her jacket."

The clerk seemed a bit taken aback and said, "Do you know her?"

I said "No, but I'd just like to pay for her jacket."

The clerk asked, "Why?"

I really didn't have an answer, other than it seemed like the thing to do at the time. If the woman was that desperate, it was the least I could do. If I could waste money on mugs that I didn't need, I could buy a jacket for someone who was in need. I expected to pay five dollars or more for the mugs, so I was still walking out with as much money as I expected to.

"Oh, this is so nice of you, I'm sure she'll want to thank you."

"No. Please, don't make a big deal out of this. Just take the money and tell her it was paid for. That's all you need to do."

She turned to the other clerk to tell her, but I didn't want a scene. I dropped the five on the counter, grabbed my mugs, and left.

One of the mugs broke during a move years later, but I still have the other. I intended to get the mugs as a reminder of home, but that remaining mug now has a very different meaning. It reminds me to do my little part when I can.

He Can't Go Home, They'll Kill Him!

ANOTHER L.A. sporting event that holds a special place in my memory is the 1994 World Cup, the later rounds, and the finals, which were held at the Rose Bowl in Pasadena. We tried to get tickets to the finals, but weren't able to get any of the rounds beyond the quarter finals. One of the games we attended turned out to be one of the most famous in World Cup history for a tragic reason.

U.S.A. vs. Colombia. Andrés Escobar came across the goal to help his goalie on defense, but accidentally deflected the ball into the net.

The Colombians sitting behind us were mortified. "Dios Mio!" "He can't go back to Colombia!" "They'll kill him!" We thought they were exaggerating as at American football games when people yell "Kill the ref!" they don't literally mean to murder the referee.

The game ended with the U.S. winning 2-1, so that own goal made all the difference.

The Rose Bowl scoreboard shows the first score in a preliminary game at the World Cup. Unfortunately for Colombia, Escobar scored it for the U.S.A.

In South America and much of the rest of the world, they take their football as a life or death matter. Escobar had not been back in Medellín two weeks before he was shot and killed. There were Colombian sports commentators who caused an international sensation by saying that this was pretty much a fitting punishment for such a mistake. That is taking sports and a mistake much too seriously.

Deuce Patrol...and More

FOR years, I taught comedy traffic school in L.A., San Diego, and Orange Counties. There will be more stories about that in **Section V**. The first traffic school I taught for in L.A. had us go on police ride-alongs to see what the enforcement of traffic laws looked like from the other side of the ticket book. We were supposed to go on one with LAPD and one with the California Highway Patrol, but I was eager to learn, and as a writer wanted to see more of how the world looked from a police car and I went on several.

For one LAPD ride-along, I was assigned to go with a Black officer. We saw a car driving very badly—speeding, running a red light (not even close to yellow)—and we pulled him over.

Before the officer could even get out of the car, the reckless driver was out of his car and charging back to the police car. On the way, the man was screaming every racial slur I have ever heard, and several I had never heard before. I think he was making them up on the spot. "You filthy f***ng n***er!" and much, much more.

The officer calmly looked up at the bigot and said, "Could I see your license, registration, and proof of insurance, please?"

I was expecting an argument about this, but the guy stormed back to his car, cursing the whole way. He came back to the police car and threw the items into the cop's chest. The cop picked them up and quiet-

The C.H.P. sergeant's car along the side of the freeway.

ly began writing the ticket while the guy stood over him continuing the stream of racist garbage. I was shocked and shaking.

I wanted to say or do something. There was the nightstick right next to me, between the seats. I looked at it, thinking: I could take it out, walk around behind the car, come up behind the guy and whack him in the back of the head. Just for the good of society. Or the shotgun. There was the shotgun right there. I could use that.

The screed kept up as the officer handed the papers back to the man and handed him the ticket book and a pen and politely said, "Please sign where the X is."

The guy did, then flung the ticket book at the cop. The cop pulled out the man's copy of the ticket, handed it to him and, without the slightest hint of sarcasm, said, "You have a nice day. Drive safely."

And he backed the patrol car up and drove away.

I was seething, and the officer was nonplussed. I was awaiting some reaction but still saw no sign his blood pressure had risen even a notch. I finally said, "I can't believe that."

He said, "What?" Then he looked at me and said, "Oh, that. Yeah. Happens all the time. At least once a day."

"And you don't say anything???"

"What would you like me to say? I'm not so brilliant that I could possibly find anything so wise and wonderful to say that it would enlighten that guy who clearly has lived his life that way. I have no delusions about educating people like that, so I just go about my day."

I said, "But doesn't it bother you…"

The officer said, "Oh, please, if I took home with me every time someone called me a stupid n***er, I'd have no life. I'm not going to let him ruin my shift, let alone my home time."

I was still shaking with rage. He added, "Let it go. You can't carry that shit around with you or it will drive you crazy."

He was right. It would. I could never have had that patience.

I did another ride-along with LAPD The officer was an older white guy who was a good bit overweight. These were the years when Daryl Gates, whose racism ran through the entire department, was Chief of LAPD I worked with some cops and ex-cops at one of the traffic schools and the things some of them said about anyone who wasn't white and straight were appalling. People were shocked when they heard some of the racial slurs from the Rodney King police radio recordings, or some of the testimony in the O.J. Simpson trial. I was not. I had heard that language from too many bigots who should never have been given badges.

LAPD and its chief had done a lot to bring grief upon themselves, and that conflict came out as we drove around the city, especially in neighborhoods where people of color lived. Residents would yell obscenities at the LAPD car. At one point someone spit on the windshield. I wanted to yell back, "Hey, I didn't do anything!"

We were driving past a Burger King and a Black kid, maybe 14 or so, threw his entire large soda at the car and it splattered all across the windshield. He added a few words of contempt for the police.

The cop kept driving. I said, "Aren't you going to do anything?"

He said, "Yep. Find a car wash."

I said, "I mean about the kid."

He said, "What would you like me to do? Stop? He'll run. I'm 53 years old and carrying 40 extra pounds. Plus another 40 pounds of Kevlar, gun belt, nightstick and all this other crap. Who do you think will win this race? I could then call for back-up and we could turn this neighborhood upside down. Do you think that will win us any friends around here? Given what these people think of cops, they won't call us for a shooting so they're sure not going to help us follow the kid. If we did catch him, which is unlikely, do you think a D.A. wants his time taken up prosecuting this?" He sighed. "I'll find a car wash."

I can't imagine putting up with that every day, but he had a point. And I certainly couldn't blame the locals for feeling the way they did. It was a sad situation.

The ride-along with the CHP was particularly interesting. I went along with a sergeant, who in addition to being a cop, was a traffic reporter on KNX, the main news station in L.A. with traffic reports every 10 minutes. I later got to visit her at the station, and it was there I got to meet L.A. traffic legend, Loyd Sigmon, inventor of the Sig Alert. It was amazing to see how hard she worked to stay updated and ready to go on the air every 10 minutes. I can't imagine the stress and pressure, and I have listened to traffic reports very differently ever since.

I ended up going on two more ride-alongs with her with the intention of writing a magazine story about her, but couldn't find a magazine that wanted the story and paid enough to be worth the effort. The time spent with her gave me quite a look at police work if I ever do want to write about it.

One night we were on what the cops called "deuce patrol," combing the freeways after 1 a.m. in search of people who were driving drunk. The old California Vehicle Code section for impaired driving was "502," and somehow that final "2" became the nickname for "deuce patrol." Strangely, we couldn't find any drunks. She said it was rare not to find anyone at all. We'd see a car swerving or driving erratically, and upon pulling them over would find the driver was lighting a cigarette, or otherwise distracted, or just a terrible driver, but there was no smell of booze, and her experienced eye and nose told her they weren't drunk. She'd cite them for speeding or failure to signal a lane change or whatever else they had done, but we couldn't find a drunk.

It was now about 2:30 a.m. and we still hadn't found anyone drunk. The sergeant said to me, "I'd really like to show you a DUI arrest before the night is over. I have never had a night like this when there are no drunks out. So from now on, if the driver isn't drunk, I'll just give them a warning and not write them a ticket so we can get moving faster and get back on patrol." She did that for the next two or three bad drivers we encountered, none of whom were drunk.

Then we saw him. A guy in a Mercedes sliding across two or three lanes with no signal and no control. Changing speed from 40 to 80. Clearly out of control.

She said, "Here we go. I'm gonna light him up."

She was behind him for a while, but he gave no indication he had noticed her. She hit the siren, something they actually don't do very often on the freeway, and almost never do in heavy traffic because it's more likely to cause confusion than clear a lane. But the freeway was almost empty. Except for us and the car that still wasn't pulling over. "He must be really drunk if he's not seeing us," she said.

She switched the types of sirens a few times before it finally caught his attention. He drove on a little while then slowly pulled to the shoulder.

We walked up to his window. He had a cell phone in his left hand and a pen in his right hand and a legal pad pressed up against the dashboard on which he was scribbling notes. He didn't look up from his note taking. The sergeant waited a moment then tapped on the glass.

He lowered the window about three inches and said, "Young lady, I am an attorney with the State of California and you just made a serious career move in stopping me. I'll be with you in a minute."

And he closed the window. She was stunned. So was I. He wasn't drunk. But he was short of hands with which to drive which explained the car's crazy maneuvers. She looked at me and said, "Remember when I said I wasn't going to write any more tickets tonight? I lied."

She went back to the highway patrol car and pulled out her ticket book, walked up to the window, and started writing. Speeding. Failure to maintain a lane. Changing lanes without signaling. Unsafe lane change (several of those).

He finally rolled down the window and started yelling how she couldn't cite him, did she know who he was, of course these tickets would never stick, he'd fight them and on and on…

She calmly repeated her request for his license, registration, and proof of insurance then calmly said if he was unwilling to comply, she could get out the handcuffs and take him in. And impound the car.

He grudgingly got out the requested materials. It was obvious he had not hung up his call. The flip phone was open on the seat, still lit up.

He said he was not going to sign the ticket. She again offered to take him to jail. He said he'd fight the ticket. And she politely said, "Of course you are free to do that. But if necessary, I will subpoena my guest to testify as to your driving." She indicated me. I smiled.

He scribbled his name on the ticket.

She said, "Now, I am going to follow you home. You will stay off the phone. You will maintain a safe speed. And you will stay in one lane at time. Is that clear?"

He glowered at her. As we walked back to the patrol car, he pulled away fast. We had to catch up. We didn't get very far, only a few exits, when we got a call that there was an accident and we had to let him go.

I learned a saying among police officers: it is almost impossible to talk your way out of a ticket, but it's really easy to talk your way into one.

On another ride-along with that C.H.P sergeant, we had pulled over a car for speeding on the 10 East just short of downtown L.A. As she was writing the driver a ticket, a car pulled up behind the C.H.P car, which was parked behind the car we were ticketing.

She looked at me and took a step sideways from the car she was ticketing. She said to me, "That is very odd. People don't stop like that. Keep an eye on him. Let me know if he moves." As she hurriedly finished writing the ticket, she kept looking back at the car that was stopped behind her own.

She gave the driver the ticket then, with her hand hovering near her gun, she warily approached the second car. She said to the driver, "Why are you stopped here? Is something wrong?"

He slurred, "No. I'm just waiting for the red light to change." He pointed to the red light on the light bar on top of her patrol car. He was so drunk he saw the red light and stopped.

The sergeant turned to me and said, "It's nice when they turn themselves in. You're finally going to get to see a DUI arrest."

Then Came the Calm Before the Storm

IT was very early on the morning of April 29, 1992. I was on a ride-along with the CHP sergeant again and there was nothing going on. I mean nothing. She kept doing radio checks thinking that she just wasn't getting the calls, but there just weren't any. We were operating out of the Culver City CHP station and she was even checking the Culver City PD and LAPD radio frequencies thinking we could go back them up if they had anything going on. They didn't.

She suggested we go to South Central L.A. She said, "There is always something happening down there." As a sergeant she was allowed to roam beyond the usual parameters of her patrol area. So off we went. And found...nothing.

We were parked on the corner of Florence and Normandy, waiting for something, anything to happen. Trying to find some action.

Then we saw it! A couple drove by and the woman in the passenger seat held a baby in her lap! Finally, a ticket to write!

The sergeant lit them up and pulled them over and explained that they were required to have the child in a proper child safety seat. The man driving immediately started yelling at the sergeant and asking if she didn't have anything better to do than harass people for something so petty. I chuckled to myself—no, honestly, we didn't have anything better to do this night.

The sergeant told him that a few nights earlier she'd had to help paramedics remove a baby's head from a windshield because the parents didn't have their kid in a child safety seat, so she really thought it was kind of important to warn them of the dangers of transporting their child this way. She said she'd make them a deal, if they promised to go out the next day and buy a safety seat, she wouldn't write them the ticket. "I'd rather you spend the money on a seat than a ticket." They were driving an older, beat-up car and it was obvious they didn't have much money, as few people in that neighborhood did.

The man chose to swear at her instead. So she wrote them the ticket. Afterward she said, "The crazy part is, he just had to calm down and promise me. I'd have no way of checking. But to get that ticket taken care of, he'll have to show a child seat in court. So he'll still have to buy the seat AND pay $400 on top of that, but it's the only way I can know for sure he's actually going to get one.

That was at the corner of Florence and Normandy where nothing else was happening. Fourteen hours later, that intersection was going to be the flashpoint for the start of the L.A. riots that followed the acquittal of the cops who beat Rodney King. Seeing that intersection on the news half a day later, it was hard to believe how calm and quiet it was the night before.

L.A. Riots

ANYONE who was alive and old enough to have a memory of 1992 remembers what happened in the wake of the not-guilty verdict in the trial of the police officers who beat motorist Rodney King. For those of us who lived in Los Angeles at the time, those memories are impossible to purge from our minds.

The rioting started in South-Central L.A. and slowly spread north to Hollywood and west toward the beaches. At first it was just something we were seeing on TV; the next morning, I could see smoke in the distance where more buildings were being set on fire. By whatever quirk of geography from my apartment, although it was only on the second floor, a block from the ocean, on a clear day I could see the skyline of downtown Los Angeles and the Hollywood sign. I needed my telephoto lens to be able to see the individual letters of the sign rather than just a white line on the hillside about 15 miles away, but it was visible.

Although barely visible from the window of my apartment in Venice, seeing the Hollywood Sign was a good reminder of why I had moved to Los Angeles.

A day later, the riots marched westward, and instead of just clouds of smoke, it was possible to see the glow of the fires. The riots had already morphed from being a protest against the verdict to general anger and frustration and, in some cases, just an excuse to loot and destroy. I still remember a reporter approaching a man who was carrying a TV out of a shattered store and asking what the man thought of Rodney King and the looter saying, "Sorry, I don't follow sports." He cared nothing about the injustice; he just wanted a free television. My two roommates and I had the TV on constantly, watching this disaster unfold in real time. As things started getting worse, they each decided to go home to their families who lived in far-flung L.A. suburbs.

The next day, as the movement shifted farther west, it was possible to see individual fires ignite in the distance. The inept response of LAPD and its incompetent, racist chief, made it clear that help would not be coming soon. The neighbors and I held a meeting. What should we do?

We discussed leaving town. I had already thought about that. I am sure either of my roommates' families would have taken me in, and I had other friends way out on the periphery of L.A. or even in the San Francisco Bay Area or Las Vegas or Phoenix to whom I could go if necessary. But that raised other questions. If I were leaving, what route would I take? If I only got to take one carload of stuff, what would it be? Clearly some clothes and essentials. My computer. But if I started piling a lot of things of value into the car, like the television, would that make me a target? There were reports of fleeing cars being stopped, the driver dragged out and beaten, their possessions stolen, and their car set on fire. That meant fleeing east toward Phoenix or Vegas or south to Orange County were out. Either route would take me through the riots. That left heading north along the coast highway. Traffic was bad and getting worse. And leaving meant abandoning my neighbors and all of my other possessions left behind. At this point, the rioters were not targeting houses or apartment buildings, just businesses. If I stayed, it would probably be okay.

The nearest business was four buildings south of my apartment: a small convenience store with exorbitant prices, run by an immigrant family. I only shopped there every few months when I was so desperate for something that I was willing to pay double or triple what I'd pay at a supermarket. For some reason, businesses owned by Asians seemed to be a particular target for the unrest. Right next to the store was an apartment building. If the store was torched, there would be no way to stop the fire from spreading to that building next door. But next to that apartment building was a gap. Maybe 40 feet wide, sort of a natural fire break.

The neighbors and I agreed to pool our resources. Who had garden hoses? We would assemble all of the hoses. Who had functioning hose taps? Where could we connect all of the hoses we had in such a way they could reach the apartment building we were willing to sacrifice? For the people who lived in the sacrificial building we'd let anyone who wanted to put their valuables in our safer apartments and we'd offer them a place to stay if their building was lost. Since it was highly unlikely the fire department would come, we'd do our best to stop the fire in that opening between those two buildings.

The news couldn't possibly keep up with the spread of the disaster, so we'd keep an eye on things ourselves. We'd stay inside and let the rioters pass by us and if they torched the store, we'd be ready to act. My apartment seemed to have the best view, so we set up a command post in my dining room window. People brought binoculars. We assembled a list of each other's phone numbers and organized a phone tree, so everyone knew who to call if we were going to have to execute the plan to fight the fire. Hoses were to be kept inside so they weren't stolen or destroyed. Everyone had to know where to find one, and which hose tap was their assigned hook up. We set a schedule so someone would be on watch 24/7.

We were supposed to sleep when not on watch, but with all of the anxiety and helicopters it was hard to sleep so I usually ended up sitting up most of the time with whoever was on watch, just attempting short naps here and there, usually unsuccessfully. Neighbors would stop by at all hours with coffee or beer. We had the TV on for the news and the classic rock radio station was still on the air providing coverage of the events.

In what could have been a radio show from the 1930s, the on-air drama was riveting. One of their DJs, to whom I had been listening for years so I felt like I knew him, had volunteered to stay and staff the station as others on their team fled as the mayhem got closer to their building. The station was part of the national emergency broadcast system and their building was fortified to withstand fires, earthquakes, and pretty much everything short of a direct nuclear hit. Once sealed, it was supposedly impenetrable. The DJ locked himself in with enough provisions to last a while. Although his usual duty was spinning rock classics, he was now also delivering the news as it came in on their wire, giving updates on the dangerously growing unrest. Overhead, their helicopter traffic reporter was giving the play-by-play as the riots got closer. Every once in a while, after hours on the air, the DJ would say something like, "I am now going to play side two of *Aqualung* and take a nap for 25 minutes." And would.

As the destruction closed in on the building, reported on by the chopper pilot, you could hear the growing fear in both their voices, but also the DJ's determination to stay on the air to provide comfort and information to Angelinos in need. As the mobs got closer, the pilot told the DJ that he really should get out of there. Already several other radio stations had been attacked and ransacked, so it was not inconceivable this one would be next. The DJ said he didn't think he had time to get away and wouldn't know which way to run. Besides, wasn't this building supposed to be a fortress against just such events?

On air, the two guys, who clearly were friends in addition to being work colleagues, discussed options. The pilot said he would hover overhead, and if it looked like the building was being breached he'd come to the roof. He made the DJ promise that at that point there was to be no argument or discussion. If he said run, he'd better run to the roof and be ready to board the chopper. There was no helipad on the roof or safe place to land, so he would hover as low as he could, and the DJ would just have to jump up on the skids and climb into the helicopter. The DJ agreed and said he'd be ready to bolt to the roof on a moment's notice. He even put on a long album side to go check the route to the roof to make sure he knew the way, how to open the access door, and scout out where on the roof the helicopter could get close without hitting antennae or air conditioning equipment.

There was real fear in the pilot's voice as he said people were trying to break into the building, but the steel security doors seemed to be holding. Then the rioters started stacking things against the door and set fire to them. They were going to try to burn the building down! The pilot again asked the DJ if it wasn't time to get out. The DJ said he was watching the action on the building's security cameras and so far, the steel was resisting the fire, but if either of them saw the building catch, he'd be up to the roof in a flash.

My neighbor and I were sitting in my apartment, yelling at the radio for the DJ to get the hell out, now! We were as frantic as the pilot and we couldn't even see what was happening.

Then the pilot said, "Shit!" something he wasn't supposed to say on the air, but under the circumstances, no one could have cared. He was almost out of fuel. He had to leave now, like right now, or he wouldn't have enough to make it safely back to the airport. He had been focused on flying cover for so long, he had lost track of the time for refueling. He said he was radioing the helicopter traffic reporter from a rival station, asking him to come and take his post. He explained what the situation was, and the competing pilot immediately agreed to zip over and fly watch over the building and the DJ until the other chopper could refuel and return.

After several attempts to enter the building or set it on fire, the rioters gave up and moved on to easier targets. The DJ's own air cover returned. He felt safe enough to try another nap knowing his pilot would wake him if anything happened. As though we weren't tense enough, listening to all that unfold just miles away had us all worked up.

By day three or four, we could see the fires much closer, and heard on the radio and TV that businesses less than a mile away from us on Lincoln Boulevard in Venice, were being set ablaze. We knew our time was coming.

Finally the police, backed now by the National Guard, went into action. They began pushing back against the rioters, and the unrest never came farther west into Venice. We could stand down.

The final toll was 63 dead. Thousands of people injured. Thousands of buildings burned.

After a good long sleep, I went out to see an armored personnel carrier parked on the sidewalk right in front of my building. I walked to the beach and was greeted by another fighting vehicle, where a man in full battle dress, manning a mounted machine gun in the top turret barked at me, "The beach is closed! Go home!"

I just wanted to get out and relax for a minute, but that was not to be. I know I should have been grateful for the armed protection, but I really resented that my neighborhood and my beach looked like a war zone.

When the chance came to fly away, I did.

Los Angeles was still under what was essentially martial law. My friend Rick and I decided we needed to get out for a bit. He belonged to a flying club based at the Van Nuys Airport and he suggested we fly up to the Santa Ynez Airport, just north of Santa Barbara. It was one

Me standing next to a plane my friend Rick rented for another of our flying adventures.

of Rick's favorite places to fly. Pretty mountains to fly over. A good restaurant at the airport and places and nice places to walk to from the airport. Many other small general aviation airports are in the middle of nowhere with not much around.

Pilots of small planes used to refer to these little jaunts as "the hundred-dollar hamburger." Meaning they spent $100 in fuel and plane rental to buy a $5 burger. These days, with the higher price of aviation fuel, it is now at least a $400 hamburger. But clearly the point of the trip was not the lunch, it was to fly and escape into the sky.

We definitely needed to get out of L.A. after watching it burn. Even though I knew the cops and National Guard were there to be helpful, I resented that my city was armed like Baghdad.

Rick and I flew to Santa Ynez. Not a long flight, not as fun as flying to Catalina or San Luis Obispo, but just what we needed. We had such a great day, wandering around and doing nothing, that we let the time get away from us and completely forgot the curfew in L.A. I don't think it was that late, maybe 8 or 9 o'clock, but we landed well after curfew.

I didn't realize that until I got on the road and there was no one in sight. I mean no one. I wasn't sure what to do. I decided to try to go home. Driving to Rick's, or other places where I had friends in the Valley, was almost as far, and just as risky as going home.

I got on the 405 Freeway, which is a parking lot during rush hour and generally packed at any other time of day, and there wasn't another car on the freeway. Not another vehicle. The freeway was empty. And it was strangely frightening. I had never seen a freeway with no cars on it. I wasn't sure what to do. I felt so alone. And vulnerable. Instead of speeding with no one around, I found myself driving slower and slower, even though there were no cops or anyone else in sight. A couple times I looked at the speedometer and found myself doing 30 mph, which still somehow seemed too fast. I tried to force myself to do at least 45, but it felt wrong. At that speed I caught up with another car, who apparently like me was having a hard time doing a real speed.

I passed the car and was almost tempted to slow down and stay with the car for company and safety, but they were only doing about 20 mph and I also didn't want to scare them and leave them wondering what I was doing, so I drove on.

It seemed to take forever for me to cover the 20 or so miles back to Venice. When I got off at the Venice Boulevard exit, there was a roadblock at the end of the off ramp. I stopped. A not very friendly cop asked what I was doing. I told him the truth about flying out of town and losing track of time. He asked to see my ID to verify this was my neighborhood. He told me to drive straight home, not to stop for red lights or stop signs. He said there would be no one else on the roads and to just get home.

I promised to do that. And I drove home. I passed maybe five police cars on the way, but none seemed to pay any attention to my running red lights. I went home and resumed what felt like house arrest.

A few weeks later, I made a trip to my favorite camera shop in Hollywood and was saddened to see it had been burned and looted. I drove past the radio station, curious to see how it withstood the siege, but other than some scorch marks on the steel exterior, it looked unscathed.

I, like many of my friends, had already been considering moving away from L.A. Some had already moved back to Pennsylvania or wherever they were from. Some to other parts of California. After having my neighborhood occupied by troops, after watching my city burn, I knew I'd never be able to look at it the same way again. When I went to the Olympics in Barcelona a few months later everyone, upon learning I lived in L.A., asked me how the riots could have happened, what was wrong with that city. When I realized I had no good explanation for this, I made up my mind that I, too, wanted to move away, and did a few months after I returned from Europe.

The Old Man and the Kite Runner

THE retired couple who lived next door to my family were probably in their late 60s (which we kids thought of as *really* old). They did not have any children in a neighborhood that was overrun with them, and they kept very much to themselves. Our house was at the top of a hill so when we were playing in our backyard, our balls would tend to roll into their yard next door. I don't recall the couple ever yelling at us, but I do recall them glowering at us from the window when some brave or hapless kid was sent to retrieve our property.

One day a friend and I pooled our meager resources to buy a kite. One of those super-cheap, flimsy ones, but it was the best we could afford. We walked the half-mile or so to Mitchell's Corners, the tiny little shopping area that predated strip malls, and paid probably all of 50 cents for the kite kit. This was also before "free-range parenting" was even a term, and we just wandered at will all day. We didn't have to be home until dinnertime and then we were allowed back out to roam until the streetlights came on. Neither we, nor our parents, gave much thought to eight-year-olds trekking out, including crossing a major street, part of U.S. Route 19, to go shopping.

We brought the kite home and assembled it. It looked much more pathetic than the picture on the package. We attached a length of string and took turns running with it, trying to get it to catch a breeze. Time after time it just nosedived into the ground. I had a brilliant idea to run down the hill toward the neighbors' yard in hopes that as I descended, the kite would have the extra lift it needed to become airborne. The kite did gain a little more altitude before swinging up and over and crashing down hard in the neighbors' yard.

My friend and I both swallowed hard. We didn't want to venture into that scary backyard. But we knew we had to retrieve our kite. We had a lot invested in it. After a brief discussion as to who should run the risk of this dangerous mission, we decided there was safety in numbers and we'd go together. We had barely stepped over the low wall dividing the yards, like prisoners crossing the deadline on the way to the perimeter fence, when the old neighbor was rushing out his door.

"Hey, you kids!"

Oh crap.

"What do you think you're doing!?" He got to the kite before we did and instantly began ripping it apart.

All we could do was watch in horror. It was his yard. It now must be his kite. Those must be the rules.

But he was disassembling the kite in an orderly fashion. He looked at us and said, "You're never going to get this in the air like this. First of all, you need to have the string attached closer to the center of gravity…" He quickly made the change. "Then, you've got to have the sheet of it bowed a bit to catch some wind. Like the sail on a sailboat." He bent the rods to create a concave kite. Then he said, "And this tail is all wrong. It has to have a little more weight to give the bottom ballast, so it flies right side up. Hold this. Wait here."

He thrust the kite at me and ran inside his house. He returned minutes later with some newspapers and some rags. The papers he folded and used to reinforce the too-thin, almost tissue-paper kite surface, which was already showing tears from its crash landings. The rags, he quickly ripped apart and tied into a tail in a fashion I had only seen in cartoons, with the bows evenly spaced down a string. While I held the kite, he attached the tail. I noticed his wife standing at their dining room window watching and beaming at the boyish delight her husband was having with this toy.

Once the alterations were complete, he took the kite from me and ran up to the top of the hill in his backyard and then came dive bombing back down the hill, letting the kite fly free behind him and…we had liftoff! It instantly soared into the air and was catching more wind and climbing. He handed the string ball to my friend and said, "Run! Keep up the speed so it will keep climbing!"

My friend did, and the kite did. The joy on the old man's face was wonderful to behold. I still get tears in my eyes thinking of that moment and his wife watching with pride from the window.

Now, far from fearing the "angry" old neighbor, we always said hello. And we suspected that if our ball landed in his yard again, the worst that could happen was he'd teach us to throw a wicked curveball.

III.
Travels
without
Charley

900

HOURS:
TUES. & THURS
WED, FRI, S
CHI
SIDE

HOME OF
Ernie Pyle
A GIFT TO THE PEOPLE
OF ALBUQUERQUE

WHEN I was in high school, I discovered the writings of Ernie Pyle. He became one of my heroes and role models. I loved his essays about his nonstop drive around the United States. For over six years, Pyle wrote six stories a week about the people and places he encountered in his wanderings. His simple style and knack for finding and drawing out interesting stories was an inspiration. He had a skill for hearing and telling the stories of everyday people and making them fascinating. He could make an old man playing checkers on the porch of a general store in Arkansas sound so interesting, you wanted to drive to the Ozarks to meet the guy for a game. When I was in college, my brother gave me a first edition of Pyle's collected essays. Pyle is best-known for his essays written during World War II, an assignment that eventually cost him his life at the hands of a Japanese sniper.

Likewise, I loved other books about extended road trips, including John Steinbeck's *Travels with Charley* and William Least Heat-Moon's *Blue Highways*. I always thought Pyle, and later, Charles Kuralt (of CBS's *On the Road*—I later learned through a mutual friend that Kuralt had also been inspired by Pyle) had the greatest jobs—crisscrossing the country to see how life was in different places, and plucking pieces of it to record and share. In the course of my travels, I wanted to visit Pyle's home in Albuquerque, his grave in Hawai'i, and Steinbeck's home and other sites related to his life and writings in Salinas and Monterey.

I've driven across the U.S. three times, and have hit 43 states in the process. I need to visit the rest of the states, and so many places that I've missed in the states I've visited. I've traveled up and down the Baja Peninsula of Mexico, inspired in part by Steinbeck's *Log from the Sea of Cortez*, and I bopped around Europe a bit. (Those stories will come in later volumes of plogs.) I still want to do much more. This section covers some of my adventures on the move.

Memories of Michoacán

THROUGH a friend of a friend, I got connected with a group that was sort of a low-budget *Earthwatch*. The idea of these groups is they would get volunteers to pay their way to assist scientists with their work. Some of the money paid would go to the group for their overhead and some to the scientist to help support their research. These trips included natural history, conservation, archeology, and other projects.

Visiting the home of one of my heroes, Ernie Pyle, in Albuquerque.

In addition to the projects covered in detail in the upcoming stories, I also participated in a dolphin census in the Sea of Cortez and an archeological dig of a stagecoach stop. I made a deal with the organization that I would pay my way to wherever the project was happening, but not pay any of the usual fees to the group. I would then turn around and write newspaper and magazine articles about the project.

While on each project, I'd make sure that I got good photos of each of the volunteers, and I interviewed those who were willing about their involvement and what they did in their professional lives. I made sure I got their contact information to follow up.

When I got back home, I'd pitch the story. Every periodical got a slightly different version of what was essentially the same article with the local person plugged in. For the *Portland Oregonian* the story was "Local Printer Saves Turtles." For the *Orange County Register*, it was "Local Photographer Saves Turtles." For the *Pittsburgh Press*, "Local School Principal Saves Turtles."

As far as I was concerned, these trips were a win-win-win-win-win. I got an amazing vacation (albeit a working vacation); the organization got publicity (after one of my articles was published, they invariably got a spike in phone calls from the area where the story ran); it raised awareness about the endangered turtles or whatever the issue was; the papers and magazines ate it up and paid me for the articles; and the individual featured in the article got kudos and love from their community. After the *Orange County Register* ran the article, the man featured in it said he had people approach him in a grocery store and in a restaurant to ask, "Hey, aren't you the turtle guy?"

The first trip I took with the group was to the Mexican state of Michoacán to work with scientists from UNAM, (The National Autonomous University of Mexico) in Mexico City, who were trying to save endangered sea turtles, primarily leatherbacks.

Leatherback turtles are beautiful creatures, one of the least-evolved large animals on earth. They show up in the fossil record pretty much unchanged since before dinosaurs walked the earth. They outlasted the dinosaurs and other great extinction events but could very well be wiped out by humans in my lifetime. There was a time when thousands of turtles a night would nest on this beach in Michoacán and now the scientists were lucky to count hundreds in an entire season.

The leatherback is by far the largest of the seven species of sea turtles. They can grow up to seven feet long, five feet wide, and weigh 1500 pounds. When they hatch they are so small I could hold four of

Holding a pair of newborn leatherback turtles. When they are full-grown, they can be over 1000 pounds which would make this a lot more difficult.

the babies in the palm of my hand. They can dive deeper than any other air-breathing animal and stay down longer. Unlike other turtles which have a hard carapace, their shells are pliable so they give, rather than crack, under the pressures of a deep dive. Their shells felt like a high school wrestling mat: I could press my finger into the shell, and slowly the indentation would smooth out and disappear.

The creatures face numerous threats, and there is only so much these scientists can do to combat the dangers. One huge problem is that the majority of a sea turtle's diet is jellyfish. A clear plastic bag floating on the surface looks just like a jellyfish from below. The turtle attempts to eat the bag and chokes to death when it gets stuck in its throat. Turtles get other types of plastic caught on them, such as six-pack holders. As the turtle grows, the plastic binds tighter and tighter often resulting in a deformed or lost flipper. Once a turtle is missing a flipper, it has a very short life expectancy.

Once a baby male turtle crawls to the sea, he never returns to land. A female returns only after several decades to lay eggs in a nest she has dug in the sand with her giant flippers. The females usually only dig nests at night, although I was lucky enough to photograph one who mistakenly came ashore during the day. That was such a rare occurrence that none of the scientists, some of whom had been working with turtles for years, had ever seen a turtle in sunlight.

The female leatherback uses her rear flippers to dig a hole in the beach about two feet deep, and then positions herself over it to deposit 30 to 40 round eggs, each about the size of a billiard ball. Her flippers then push sand over the eggs and tamp it down. The entire time she is doing this, it looks like she is crying. They are not real tears, but moisture secreted to protect her eyes from getting sand in them. Her eyes are usually covered with water so can dry out quickly when exposed to the air.

While the turtle is nesting, she enters a trance of sorts and won't even flinch when we used a device, like a giant version of the gun used for ear piercing, to tag her flipper. The plastic disk we attached had information about the project and encouraged anyone who found the turtle to report the location, date, tag number, and other pertinent information as part of an international project to track the turtles across their global range. A great deal is still unknown about the turtles, due to their pelagic nature. Their life expectancy may be 30 years or over

The scientists kept a collection of some of the illegal products that contributed to the endangered status of the turtles.

100. I got to tag three turtles and I would like to think *my* turtles are still out happily cruising the oceans.

There is another challenge to the turtles' continued existence: poachers. Around the world the eggs are valued as a delicacy, and in some places, including Mexico, as an aphrodisiac. One egg can be worth the equivalent of $1 U.S. In a region of Mexico where many people only earn $60 to $100 a month, a couple of clutches of stolen eggs could double someone's income, so the scientists are not unsympathetic as to why people would put feeding their families ahead of saving an endangered species. Not only are the eggs stolen, but the turtles themselves are killed for their oil and the other products that can be made from them. Mexico and many other countries have banned the sale of eggs and other turtle products, but the laws are often ignored. In the town near the beach, turtle products were sold openly. I was told that in the local bars, poachers were selling eggs to people who would crack the eggs and eat their contents raw, right from the shell.

One of the jobs of the volunteers was to try to get to the turtles before the poachers did. If possible, we'd use a bag to catch the eggs as they dropped out of the mother. If we got there a little late or the

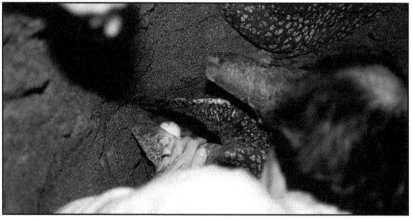

Volunteers work to retrieve the eggs as a mother turtle deposits them in the nest she just dug.

eggs missed the bag, we'd scoop them out of the hole before the mother backfilled it. We would then rebury the eggs in a compound ringed with barbed wire and guarded by heavily armed members of the Mexican Navy, Los Marinos. The Marines presented their own dangers, but that part of the story comes later.

One of the most amazing things—and there were many on this trip—was the bubbling of the turtles to the surface when they hatched.

If anyone was around to see it when it started, they would alert everyone else and we'd run to the compound to watch the sand start to boil. We wanted to watch the fascinating phenomenon, but also needed to be there to protect the turtles from birds and other threats that would immediately present themselves. I wish someone had a video camera to have recorded this incredible phenomenon. (There are videos on YouTube of the nesting and hatching process. It is amazing to see, and even more incredible in person.)

Sometimes a baby turtle straggler would come out hours or days after the rest of his brothers and sisters. Its chances of surviving were minimal. If the turtles made their way to the surface during the day, the sun was hot, and the sand was scalding, so the hatchlings would often burn up on their way to the water. To spare them that fate, if a clutch hatched during the day, we'd gather them into a bucket of water and keep them in the shade to be released at night after the sand had cooled sufficiently.

In addition to the heat, the tiny turtles had to run a gauntlet of hungry seagulls and crabs as they made their way to the water, and then risked being eaten by fish as soon they were in the ocean.

Before scientists discovered the error of their ways, they used to release the hatchlings by pouring the bucket of turtles directly into the ocean, sparing the babies the beach walk. The problem that didn't become known until many years of babies had been released that way, was that the turtles never touched their beach of birth. Somehow, in a mysterious process that no one has yet deciphered, the turtle learns the sand of its home. As it makes its way to the water, that beach imprints on the baby.

Experiments have been done where a turtle, either a baby or adult, has been put in a room with areas of sand collected from different parts of the world and the turtle will check out the various sands until it finds the sand from the beach of its birth. A turtle can somehow sense the right sand from the beach where it hatched and made its run to the ocean. A turtle from our beach in Michoacán could tell the difference between the sand from its beach and that from another Mexican beach 100 kilometers north. An Indonesian turtle knows its sand and won't sit down on Costa Rican sand. Turtles who were placed in the water and never got to imprint their beach, would just wander around that room and never find a sand onto which to settle. No one knows what happened to those lost souls who were dropped in the ocean. Do they wander the seas forever, never nesting anywhere? Turtles that were tracked have never turned up nesting on the "wrong" beach. That is, you'll never find a Florida sea turtle nesting in Madagascar. And the turtles do roam widely. Turtles tagged by the UNAM group on the west coast of Mexico have been found dead on beaches in Australia, and have been caught in fishing nets off the coasts of Wales and Cuba.

To allow the turtles to imprint their home and try to save them from being an easy dinner for a crab or seagull, we would set up a safety corridor at night and keep guard over the hatchlings as they made their way to the water, lining the route to keep away predators. If a turtle strayed too far, we'd gently steer it back onto our route. The turtles usually headed straight to the water. Again, no one knows what guides them, but they seem to know where to go. The turtles that had been kept in buckets until nightfall were released with their birth group and allowed to make their way to the sea. We'd also guard them into the water as deep as we could still stand, to discourage fish from making our babies their dinners, but beyond the breakers the little things were on their own. No one knows with any certainty, but it was estimated that maybe one baby out of a clutch of 50 eggs might survive the first 24 to 48 hours in the water. They were such defenseless targets, they were easy pickings. Not good odds for trying to save an endangered species.

It is such a tragedy that a magnificent creature that has been around so long will likely be wiped out by humans in a hundred years. These scientists in Mexico and around the world are doing their best to give them a fighting chance at survival.

As one of the few young, strong men on this expedition, I somehow got assigned most of the work of digging the ersatz nests. Using a post-hole digger and a shovel, I would dig a hole about two feet deep and wide enough to bury a basketball. The trip spanned late December and the first part of January, but it was warm that far south in Mexico, and it was hot and sweaty work. When it came time to dig a pit for a new latrine—a hole big enough for a 50-gallon drum, that duty somehow fell to me as well. I didn't mind, I was in good shape and enjoyed the workout.

(Side note along the lines of being the young, strong one: I am not the bravest guy on the planet and will admit that. If someone else is willing to take the lead on an adventure, I am okay being a loyal follower. One day about six of us were out exploring the area and we came across a cave. We all agreed it would be fun to check it out. Then everyone just stood there. I looked around our little group and realized they were all looking at me. There were three senior citizens, a teenage girl, and one of the group's employees with whom I was trying to get-together with (and eventually did, so I had to try to impress her with my bravery). As the most able-bodied person amongst us, they all expected me to go into the cave first. There was no graceful way out of this, so I had to. With only one flashlight amongst us and no idea what we might run into, I was not as disappointed as the others seemed to be to find the cave only went about 50 feet, and we had to abandon the adventure.)

Every night at dark, we'd go out patrolling the beach, looking to find the nesting turtles before the poachers did. We'd see the poachers in the distance in the dark, lurking near the tree line. In addition to the grocery bags into which they'd collect any eggs they found, many also carried machetes, so it was a little scary. One night, while we were all out on patrol, the poachers left a slaughtered turtle at the entrance to our little research palapa, (an open-sided building with a roof of palm leaves), as a sort of warning. We felt fortunate they had not trashed the scientific equipment or destroyed the semi-outdoor laboratory. Another night, they set fire to the brush around our camp, but the rancher on whose property we were camped quickly extinguished the flames with the help of his children.

Another aside about that rancher. The organization paid him to use a portion of his land, and we camped under tall coconut palm

A typical home in Caleta de Campos.

The beautiful setting for our tents in the turtle camp. The scientists' research palapa is at the right. The beach and ocean were at my back as I took this photo.

trees. His boys use to scamper up those trees in defiance of gravity to bring down coconuts. The rancho belonged to Pedro Moreno Salazar. On his gate, in giant wrought-iron letters were his initials. None of us spoke good enough Spanish to be able to explain why we giggled every time we drove onto his property past where it said P.M.S. Those initials don't have quite the same meaning in Spanish.

I arrived just after Christmas 1989 and stayed for two weeks. The scientists had been there over Christmas and still had their cute little improvised tree decorated. I'd be welcoming in the New Year there. On December 31, some of the volunteers and staff took the drive to the little coastal village of Caleta de Campos. Someone knew about a restaurant right on the beach where we ended up eating a few times during the weeks I was there. The dinners were about $4, which might have been a lobster with a side of rice and beans, and chips and salsa. I'm a much bigger fan of shrimp than lobster, so for about $4, I would get a plate of garlic shrimp so large I had a hard time finishing it, and had to share with my new friends—and that is saying a lot, because anyone who has ever been with me to a casino buffet that has peel and eat shrimp has seen me devour a lot. As I recall, beers were about 50 cents; sangria and margaritas were about $1. If we didn't have so much work to do and it weren't several miles down the road, we'd probably have eaten there every night. There was a bar of sorts, walking distance just outside the gates of our camp, also with cheap drinks, but it was not great food at ridiculously cheap prices.

Turtles only nest for a few weeks so, holiday or not, we still had to get back and do our patrols, save the eggs and rebury them in the compound. When we got back to the camp, the young marines who were supposed to be guarding the turtles and the camp were already drinking to get an early start on their New Year's celebration. They still had their large automatic rifles slung over their shoulders while doing shots. It was a little disconcerting.

We had work to do and we headed out to the beach. A couple hours later, my patrol partner and I heard a faint POP POP POP POP

Three of the scientists going with the two of heavily-armed Navy men to investigate a problem with the poachers.

POP. My companion dragged me up the beach and pushed me down behind a rock. He was a Vietnam vet who recognized the sound of incoming gunfire. We could see the splashes of bullets hitting the water. We hoped they were not hitting any turtles, but in the immediate moment all we could do was stay hidden until the shooting subsided, which it did after a few minutes. We checked our watches. It must have been Los Marinos way of ringing in the New Year at medianoche. As for me, I rang in 1990 cowering behind a rock, wondering if I would live to see any of the new year. I learned gunfire sounds very different on the receiving end of it than it does in the movies.

We did our patrols and found a few turtles. Most nights we were lucky to find 10 or 15. Some nights there were as few as three. A sad reduction from the photos the scientists had of this beach in the 1940s, when it would have been possible to walk a few kilometers on the backs of nesting turtles without your feet ever having to touch sand.

When we got back to the palapa, one of the young ladies who was working for the group was sitting inside wide-eyed and clutching a large cooking knife. While everyone was gone from camp, she had been starting preparations for the New Year's feast the next day. Apparently, the drunken marines had gotten way too grabby and she began to fear the worst. We were all relieved that things didn't go any further, and it was resolved that none of the women would ever be left alone in camp or with a marine ever again.

As far as being left alone with anyone, there was one person I didn't mind being alone with. I was not even out to myself yet, and to this day I have terrible gaydar. But I was pretty sure one of the male Mexican scientists was hitting on me. And as nervous as it made me, I liked that he was. One night in particular, he and I were on patrol and saw a turtle emerging from the sea. I had learned the routine that he had been practicing for years of doing this mission. We would stay near the turtle, trying not to get close enough to frighten it into aborting its nesting mission. We'd stay with the turtle as it went into its trance and used its massive powerful flippers to dig a hole and lay its eggs.

That night, we had the slowest turtle I had seen that entire trip. Not that I totally minded, given that we had nothing else to do and I had good company. The scientist knew little English and we were pretty dependent on my less-than-fluent Spanish. As we sat there in the warm night, shirtless under the canopy of constellations, we fell into easy, if limited conversation and things started to seem very romantic. Even more so when he leaned close to me, pointed out shooting stars, and asked me if I knew the Spanish word for them. I did not. I still think of him when I remember the *estrellas fugaces*.

The stars were another wonderful thing about patrolling all night. So many stars. No surrounding light to spoil the view. I knew the earth rotated. Heck, I even had taken a class in astronomy in college, so I was not completely ignorant of the heavens. But until I walked the beach in total darkness night after night after night, I never really got the big picture of how the earth moved through space. Constellations were clearly visible and I could watch them rise, ride across the sky, and set. I could clearly picture the planet slowly revolving through space. I've been a Libra my entire life, but I had never been anywhere dark enough to actually be able to make out the constellation. I saw the Southern Cross for the first time ever. It was amazing to see so far into space, so many stars going on forever.

We pretty much flipped our days and nights, working all night and sleeping from sunup until noon or so. A couple of days, I had things to do during the day so I tried to sleep at night. It was one of those nights while I was drifting off to sleep that I heard one of the most intriguing things I have ever heard. I had to ask the rancher the next day what the sound was. Jaguars, calling to each other in the hills above his ranch. What a haunting sound.

When one of the workers for the organization had to drive to the airport to pick up more volunteers for the second week, she wanted someone to go with her for company, to keep her awake on the three or four hour drive, and for a little added sense of security. She had a few little errands to run on the way, so I got to see some of Morelia, the capital city of Michoacán. That is where I found the shops illegally and openly selling turtle products. I always wanted to go to new places, meet new people, and see new things, whenever there was a chance to go exploring I would. It meant I got to see a few things I otherwise would have missed.

One day, one of the researchers had to visit someone they knew in the surrounding countryside, and again I volunteered to go along and was rewarded with some of the most "National Geographic-y" photos I have ever taken. An old woman's face spoke volumes of her rich, but difficult life. Near the woman's place, we had to go off into the jungle a bit and there I saw a beautiful Mexican boy sitting under a tree, weaving a hat. I wanted to sneak up on him and take a photo before he saw me and moved. I always asked permission to take someone's photo, but sometimes did it after I shot so as not to ruin the un-posed mood. I wanted to capture this perfect moment of innocence uncontaminated by the outside world. Before I could snap the photo, the boy looked up at me, and I saw his Oakland Raiders T-shirt. Before I could even register the disappointment of that, he said, in perfect, unaccented English, "Hey, what's up?" I was startled. As we talked, he explained that he had an uncle who lived in California who he visited often, hence the T-shirt and the English. You can't even go to a remote Mexican forest and not run into pieces of the United States. So much for my National Geographic cover. I didn't even bother taking that photo.

There were so many photogenic locals who were nice enough to allow me to take their pictures.

The scientists asked no one use a camera flash around a mother turtle so as not to startle it and possibly disturb its nesting. I bought special, super-high ISO film to be able to shoot in almost total darkness, but the trade-off there is that the photos are grainy, and I had to stay very still and hope the turtle didn't move. Because of those imitations, good clear photos of leatherbacks are rare and several times when one of my articles ran, I would get contacted by someone wanting to buy the rights to the photos for some other media. Some of my photos ended up in *MD Magazine*, a calendar, and best of all, I got a call from the Smithsonian asking to use my photos. I made thousands of dollars

A rare shot of a turtle nesting in broad daylight.

from the photos alone, aside from what I was paid for the articles. My photos from this and other expeditions were also licensed for a book called *Environmental Vacations*, including one on the cover.

A note of caution about the following story.
There are a few disturbing moments. Reader discretion is advised.

New Year's Day was cause for major celebration in our camp and the nearby community. Some of it was fun, some was disturbing.

As it was explained to me, New Year's was one of the few holidays the rural locals observed that was not centered around religion and family, as Christmas and Easter were. It was one of the few days when no one had work, or had to go to church, or had any obligations. The day was all about drinking and having fun. A big part of the fun in that village was a cockfight. Although the idea repulsed me, I felt I had to at least check it out. I watched one fight and left. I couldn't take anymore even though the fights were to go on all afternoon.

As an outsider, it seems wrong to judge other people's cultures, but it was more brutal than even I had imagined. It's a fight to the death. Razor sharp spurs were strapped to the birds' legs to inflict maximum damage and cause a lot of bleeding. The barbarity is hard to even think about. As the feathers became so soaked with blood, the owner of the cock would stick the bird's head in his mouth and suck off the blood to clear off its eyes to continue the fight. It was disgusting to watch.

Usually the winning cock is so badly injured that the bird also has to be killed. With little else to entertain them, the local workers really got into the fight. Several times I was asked if I wanted to bet on the outcome of a match. There were several people making book and handicapping the fights. Even if I understood how the fights worked or which cock was likely to be the best fighter, I wouldn't have wanted to participate. But the locals bet, and bet a lot. According to some of my new Mexican friends, who also declined to bet, the amount of money being bet was ridiculous. Equivalent to several month's pay. One man reportedly bet—and lost—his pickup truck. The only vehicle he owned. I can't imagine how he'd tell his wife.

I wanted to get away from the bloodshed, so I wandered up the main road. There, covered up in the road, was a recently killed pedestrian, blood still oozing from under the blanket. Apparently the man, staggering across the one main road through the small town, walked in front of a pickup truck, and was struck and killed by a drunk driver leaving the cockfight fiesta. There were five or six people standing around. I wanted to get away from bloodshed, not see more of it, so I turned back toward the fiesta and had only gone a few hundred yards when I heard a loud crash. I went back up the hill and saw another car had slammed into the back of the pickup, sending the pickup flying into the assembled little group, killing two of them. The car had gone off the road on the far side and rolled down the hill, ejecting the driver who was also killed. There were now four dead men in the space of just a few minutes. Seeing that there wasn't anything to be done about the accident—I have no medical training and the few locals on the scene were handling it—I went back down the hill. There seemed to be death and pain at both ends of my journey. I didn't have a car to go back to our camp and it was too far to walk.

As I passed the cockfighting ring, trying to find a quiet place to sit and drink, one of the sea turtle scientists asked me what was wrong. He could see how distressed I was. I told him about the accident and the four dead men up by the road. He said he knew. Word had drifted down to the crowd around the cockfighting ring. I asked if they would cancel the fight and the fiesta because of what happened. He said no. In fact, the people who relayed the news had been careful not to say who had been killed. It was likely everyone at the party knew the men and if they found out who they were, they would be too upset to enjoy the fiesta. He said, "They only have one day for this party. Those men will still be dead tomorrow and there will be plenty of time to grieve. Right now, they want to have fun." I was shocked by their priorities: valuing a cockfight over the lives of their friends. Again, I tried not to judge the local customs by what I was used to, but it was hard. I went off by myself to drink, out of sight and earshot of the fiesta.

Meanwhile, back at the ranch, for our New Year's Day party, the staff of the organization had bought a whole pig from our rancher-host and they were slow-cooking it over a pit, with an apple in its mouth and everything. I think this was the first time I had ever seen that done in person. Apparently, it's an honor to be selected to eat the pig's brain directly out of its skull. That honor somehow fell upon probably the most eccentric of the volunteers in the group. As soon as I met him, I asked him if he was any relation to a famous millionaire who had his same name and he said yes, that was his great-uncle. Giving the odd history of his famous great-uncle, this guy's odd traits should not have been surprising.

This guy arrived for a two-week stay in Mexico carrying a brown paper lunch bag. That was his entire luggage. In that bag he had one change of underwear, a toothbrush, a spoon, and a Styrofoam coffee cup. That was it. The fees the volunteers paid were not cheap, so I knew he couldn't be as destitute as his shabby attire and lack of luggage made him appear. And he came from a very wealthy family. The only time I ever saw him eat a meal not out of that Styrofoam cup was when he ate the brain of the pig out of its cranium. (For the record, I am very glad I was not selected for this honor. I almost threw up watching it, and certainly would have puked if I had eaten it.)

For every meal, Mr. Millionaire Heir would take his food and mash it into the cup. Eggs, bacon, toast for breakfast, he'd smash it all in there together with his bare hand then eat it with his spoon. When we went out for tacos, he'd mush them all into his cup and eat them with his spoon. He was probably in his late 70s, but still quite spry, and one of the hardest workers among the volunteers. He also had so many quirks, it was impossible to figure him out. There is the old saying that poor people are *crazy*; rich people are *eccentric*. He was definitely eccentric.

Among the other interesting volunteers was a guy who had been on one of the Navy ships off Bikini Atoll during the testing of nuclear bombs there. His ship was one of those that was so close that it rode

One of the volunteers had the honor—if you can call it that—of eating the pig's brain.

up on a wave created by a blast and shows up in some of the famous photos of those events surfing away from the explosion. Many of his shipmates had died of cancer and other radiation-related illnesses. He got regular checkups and was still fine, but figured he was on borrowed time and he wanted to live life to the fullest until his number was up. He would travel, seek out new adventures and make the most of it.

Between the experience with the turtles, the *estrellas fugaces*, and interesting mix of people on this trip, it still stands out as one of the most wonderful adventures of my life.

I wanted to stay a couple more days in Mexico. So did a few of the other volunteers. They all booked rooms at the Holiday Inn in Ixtapa. I got a room in Zihuatanejo, the twin city of Ixtapa. It was much, much

A street in Zihuatenejo with its open-air market.

cheaper in Zihuantanejo, but in addition to price considerations, I wanted to feel like I was staying Mexico. A Holiday Inn in Mexico looks pretty much the same as one in Los Angeles or Pittsburgh. You could not have mistaken my hotel for anything you'd find in any other place. I did go meet the volunteers poolside at their hotel bar one day for a drink, but the rest of time I went off and explored on my own. Then I flew back to California to write my articles.

Adventures in Baja

O N many of those trips, I went to Los Angeles. I met Tony and Beti on the trip to Michoacán working with the leatherback turtles. They were research scientists for the Mexican government and ran a turtle research center in the tiny fishing village of Bahia de Los Angeles. This L.A. was about as different from the one where I lived as could exist on the same planet.

They kept up to 20 sea turtles in captivity, and people came from all over the world to work with the various species there. (Sea turtles, being pelagic, are difficult to study in the wild.)

Me (on the right) working with another volunteer to move a turtle to clean and weigh it.

My then-roommate in Venice, California, along with some friends and his brother had been going to Baja to surf and to fish since they were in high school. After meeting the Mexican scientists, I had another reason to go. I met a man on another project for the group who also wanted to start going down more, so between him and my roommate's group, I made quite a few trips over the space of a few years. I tried to find articles to write to pay for my trips, and started freelancing regularly for an English-language magazine that catered to Americans who traveled to Baja. I always came back from my adventures with more stories. I even bought a four-wheel-drive SUV and equipped it to be able to explore further afield.

There were so many wonderful memories of the trips to Baja and a few scary ones. So many interesting characters and beautiful places.

The Hermit of Desengueño

DESENGUEÑO is the Spanish word for disillusionment and that seemed a very appropriate name for a played-out mining village which had become a ghost town. On one of my many visits with Tony and Beti, they took me to visit their friend, the hermit of Desengueño.

The hermit of Desengueño in front of his house in his private camp in his private town.

The town had about one hundred inhabitants when the copper mine was producing. In the 1930s, the Great Depression dropped the price of copper so low it was no longer worth operating the mine and it shut down for years. During World War II, the demand for copper shot up and suddenly the ore was worth pulling out of the ground again. When the war ended, the mine again stopped being worth the effort, and everyone left town. Well, everyone except Elian. He had lived alone in the town since 1946.

In addition to Tony and Beti, a few other people would come to see him and bring him provisions now and then. Failing a visit from someone, he snared rabbits, he knew which cacti were edible, and had a spring nearby for water. For a wider variety in his diet, he was dependent on friends and relatives. Tony suggested what we might take to Elian and, in what might be the best deal since the trade for Manhattan Island, we exchanged a large can of coffee and a carton of Marlboros for bolo ties made of silver and turquoise. I wondered about the inequality of the swap, but Elian said he finds the silver and turquoise and trades it to some Native Americans who do the silversmithing and trade him back the finished products, which he then trades for food, cigarettes, and coffee. He has plenty of silver, copper and turquoise, but they have no value if you can't eat them. Years later, I asked a jeweler friend to look at the bolo tie and he estimated it was about $300 of precious metal and semi-precious stone. I still have the tie safely packed away; sadly I rarely find occasion to wear it.

Elian showed us around his house and his town. His house was a mishmash of sticks from cacti, canvas, car parts, corrugated metal, 50-gallon drums, odd pieces of wood and fabric. He poached what he could from the remnants of the town, very little of which was still standing.

He still went down the mine occasionally, a proposition that was too scary for me to want the tour of that looming death pit. Elian was so weathered from his life outdoors, it was hard to place his age. Even if he was 20 when the mine shut down, he'd have had to have been at least 65 now, but something about his movements made me think he was closer to 80. But he was a spry old man so it was hard to tell.

He didn't have a coffee maker, or electricity to run one for that matter, so he makes his coffee every morning by grinding the grounds into the bottom of his metal cup as he pours in water heated over his fire. After he drank the liquid, he flung the grounds out of the cup and there, an arm-throw's distance from his fireside, was a heap of more than 40 years of coffee grounds. Across the fire circle the other way, also an arm-throw's distance, was a pile of cans 40, years in the making. He would heat a can over his fire—the actual can, cooking beans or corn or whatever in the can in which it came. Then he'd eat it out of the can, and when he was done, fling the can into the can pile without standing up from the fire. With a limited supply of water, it did save washing pots and dishes. All he had to clean up was a spoon.

He kept very busy, scouring the area for valuable resources, whether in the form of food, or minerals that he could trade for food. It was a simple existence, but he seemed much more content than most people I know who can jump into a car and drive to a grocery store to replenish any time they want.

I asked why he didn't go into town and he replied, "I've been there." It's hard to argue with the simplicity of that statement. He did seem happy.

I have met a lot of quirky characters both in Baja and the rest of the world, but Elian still stands out as someone who lived life completely on his own terms. He ate his meals when and how he wanted to. He answered to no one. He expected nothing and was grateful for what came his way.

On a subsequent visit, Tony and Beti told me that as Elian's health got worse, relatives forced him to move in with them in town. He didn't want to. He was perfectly okay with dying as he had lived, alone in his own domain. He did die in town, in civilization, if that is what it is. I am not sure going out that way made him happy.

The uneven exchange rate we found in Desengueño reminded me of another Baja adventure. Some friends and I were camping on a re-mote stretch of beach that took hours of hard off-roading to access. It took quite a bit of scouting and analyzing of topographical maps to get to this beach and once there, given its pristine nature, we speculated that we might be the first people to ever set foot on this sand. Usually beaches are picked clean of worthwhile flotsam and jetsam by the first people to come across the pretty shells or rocks or man-made items of interest. Who knows when anyone had last been to this beach. There were no signs of recent human visitation and nothing had been collect-ed. There was a full dolphin skeleton. Many interesting seashells. A sea lion skeleton. Several of the beautiful glass Japanese fishing net floats, clearly quite old and hand-blown.

We had not been there long and had just finished setting up camp when we saw a ponga, a small Mexican fishing boat, coming at us from way out on the Sea of Cortez. On board the ponga were four sun-worn Mexican fishermen, a few looked like they were still in their teens. They spoke no English and told us in Spanish that they had seen us on the beach and wondered if our boat had broken down and we were stranded. They had never seen anyone on this stretch of land, ever. We pointed to where our 4-wheel-drive trucks were a little ways inland, parked behind a hummock. We had not wanted to bring them onto the very soft sand of the beach out of concern they might be too hard to get out after they had sunken in for a few days. We'd had that problem be-fore and learned that carrying the tents and camping gear a few yards was easier than digging out a vehicle.

We thought it was very nice of the fishermen to detour from their work to come and make sure we were okay. They were ready to rescue us if need be. We assured them that for remote adventures like this one, we always brought two vehicles in case one broke down, so we'd probably be okay.

As we visited with them, one of the younger fishermen noticed the package of *Chips Ahoy* that we had just pulled out. The fisherman's eyes grew wide. "Galletas!" He exclaimed. We said yes, we had cookies. He said they had been camping on an island for weeks while they were fishing. They had run out of all the fun foods and were sick of eating fish. Would we like to trade for the cookies? We could see they had a boatful of fish and, although I didn't like fish, all of my companions did and were planning on catching our dinner.

(Side note about my dislike of seafood. I did eat a lot of it in Baja. It tastes so much better when it is so fresh from the water to the fire. It doesn't taste "fishy" at all.) But the fishermen did have lobsters.

On previous trips, our guys had caught lobsters, but only one or two a day. They were much harder to procure than the many other good-eating fish in the Sea of Cortez. Soon a deal was struck with our new Mexican friends. The package of *Chips Ahoy* and a jar of salsa for five lobsters—one for each of us for dinner. Not a bad deal. But again, the value of something is what it is worth to you at that moment. If you are sick of eating seafood, cookies are worth more than lobster. For the rest of our week there, whenever the ponga would go by, far out at sea, the fishermen would stand up and wave and we'd wave back.

One thing about finding things on the beach. Whenever we would camp in Baja, the first thing I would do was walk the beach with a bag and fill it full of trash. Cans, bottles—both plastic and glass—dolls, packing materials, grocery bags, all sorts of debris that had been dropped by careless people, or more likely here, washed ashore.

One of the guys was a friend of a friend and we didn't know each other that well. On about our third trip together, he asked me why I did that. He said, "Why bother? You can't single-handedly clean up Mexico."

I told him I knew that and wasn't trying to, but said, "If everyone who came down here would do this—take out one more bag of trash than they brought in, the few jerks leaving their garbage would be so outnumbered by the people cleaning up the beach, that it would always be clean." And that has always been my philosophy of life. The world doesn't need a lot of superheroes. But if everyone did just five or 10 percent more than their share of anything, the world would be a better place and we'd more than make up for the one percent of jerks trying to make it crappy.

Another interesting moment from this trip. The weather was so perfect, we slept out under the stars, on top of our sleeping bags. No need for any sort of covering. It was so relaxing to enjoy nature with nothing but swim trunks on. It was so wonderful to go to sleep looking up at the stars, including the occasional *estrellas fugaces*. With no extraneous light, it was hypnotic, and more and more stars, constellations, and galaxies came into view the longer I stared. The lapping of the waves at the shoreline a few yards away was the only sound to lull me to sleep. Paradise.

A few hours later, I was awakened by hot air entering my nostrils. What the hell? I lay there trying to sort out what was happening. What was going on? Something or someone was breathing into my nose! I froze. I wanted to open my eyes to look, but was also terrified at what I might find. I knew I had to look. Before I died, I at least had to know what was going to chew my face off.

Summoning all the courage I could, I began to slowly open my eyes, then they popped full open as I realized what it was. A coyote was sniffing my face! About two inches from my nose was his nose. I screamed. Perhaps louder than any scream I have ever let loose in my life. I scared the coyote. He leapt straight up, about six feet in the air. His little legs were pumping in midair like his cousin Wile E. in the cartoons when he runs off a cliff and it takes him a beat to realize there is no longer ground underneath him. When the frightened animal hit the ground right next to me, he was already in full flight.

The other guys woke up to my scream in time to see him literally high-tailing it down the beach. My friends understood both my and the coyote's alarm, and didn't much mind being awake in the full dark of night to once again enjoy the expanding heavens. He must have warned his coyote friends that they would be deafened by the odd creatures on the beach if they went down there, and we didn't see hide nor hair of coyotes again that trip.

The Lost Boy

THIS incident haunts me to this day. Did I do the right thing? Should I have done more? It was 30 years ago, so it's too late now, but I do wonder how this story came out in the long run.

I had written so many letters to my girlfriend in England about Baja that on one of her visits to me in Los Angeles, California, she wanted to go with me and see why I was so enamored of the place. Since mail service was slow to Bahia de Los Angeles and phone service non-existent, it was often difficult, if not impossible, to tell Tony and Beti I was coming, so my then-girlfriend (who I affectionately referred to as "The Limey") and I just drove down to Baja California and showed up at the turtle camp in Bahia.

Tony and Beti were nowhere to be found. Their nearest neighbor was a fisherman by the name of Miguel who looked after the turtles in their absence, and I went to him to ask about Tony and Beti. Miguel told me Tony and Beti had gone to Mexico, D.F., to visit Tony's family and do some work at UNAM for a few weeks. But Miguel assured me (as had Tony on earlier trips) that Tony would want me to make myself at home, so we set up camp under the palapa near Dr. Bartlett's trailer.

Dr. Bartlett was an American medical researcher who had set up a lab and trailer at Tony's. He had made several major discoveries about human blood and circulatory systems based on studying sea turtles. (Strangely, the systems are similar). Bartlett had died and left his truck, lab, and trailer to Tony for visiting scientists to use, and on various trips to Bahia, I met researchers from Brazil, Israel, Ireland, Sweden, and elsewhere who had come to use the lab and study turtles (either for the turtles' sake or for what they could tell us about humans). Tony and Beti's research camp attracted such a mix of people from all over the world, I wouldn't have surprised to run into the Prime Minister of Belgium or a U.S. senator there.

We were far enough from civilization that the Limey and I quickly stripped down and went for a quick swim in the crystal clear Sea of Cortez and then re-enacted a certain scene from the movie *From Here to Eternity*. Then we put on swim suits and were sitting on beach chairs placed in the Sea of Cortez so that only our heads were out of the water (to breath and drink Coronas). It was very hot, close to a hundred degrees, I'm sure, it being July in Baja. We heard a truck pull up. I got out of the water and walked around to see who had parked on the road on the other side of Dr. Bartlett's trailer.

I recognized Miguel's truck. He got out, as did a Caucasian kid about 10 years old who held in his arms a Cocker Spaniel puppy. The boy and dog both looked quite scared, and the boy had obviously been crying. Miguel, who doesn't speak English, said to me in Spanish, "Is this boy saying what I think he is saying?"

I replied, "What is he saying?" and turned to the boy and asked him what was up. The boy, who said his name was Peter, was barefoot and wore only shorts. His shoulders were sunburnt. He told me that he and the dog had been, according to his father, misbehaving, so the father put them out of the car to walk for a while until they settled down.

The father drove off. After waiting for what the boy said seemed like hours, he started walking and after walking quite a while he spotted Miguel's house and went there for help.

We immediately gave the boy and dog water. The dog lapped up four large bowls of it. Peter drank several glasses and ate a few granola bars while the Limey put lotion on his sunburnt shoulders and we tried to calm him down.

Peter seemed sure his father had just driven off to scare him and then got lost. Or maybe had decided to abandon him in Mexico and just leave. He seemed to waver between these two extreme ideas of where his father was. We decided to try to find the father. Miguel and Peter and the dog and I got into his truck.

My British girlfriend walking the beach near our camp in Bahia de los Angeles after we helped the American boy find his father.

We left the Limey at the camp. I told her that if the father came back to make him wait, we would check back periodically. I told her I felt bad about leaving her alone, in a foreign country where she didn't speak the language. But I told her I needed to do this and hoped she understood. I gave her the keys to my car and told her if she got scared to either lock herself in or drive over to Miguel's and see his wife, and I pointed the way.

I asked Peter if he knew where his father was headed, and he said he didn't. I asked if he had heard him mention any places and started naming popular camping and fishing spots nearby. He said Punta la Gringa sounded sort of familiar, so we headed off that way, down the beach, finding someone every kilometer or so. The bay is very pretty, and a popular spot for both gringos and Mexicans to go and camp on relatively open stretches of sand. Miguel would ask the Mexicans, and I the Americans, if they had seen a red pickup towing a brown pop-up trailer. No one had.

I could see Peter getting nervous. He was sure he would be stuck for the rest of his life in a country where he knew no one and didn't speak the language. I tried to reassure him that I knew all the Americans who lived in the area, and Miguel knew all the Mexicans, and that we would find his father. It was only a matter of time until word spread. I asked Peter if his mother was back in the states, to which he replied that he didn't have a mother. I wasn't sure if she was dead or had just split, but just the question got him crying, so I didn't pursue it.

I asked about other relatives, and he said he had grandparents in Sacramento. I assured him that if we couldn't find his father in a couple of days that I would take him with me back to the U.S., call his grandparents, and get him to them. We would not turn him over to the Mexican authorities. Miguel and I discussed that possibility in Spanish, and although he knew the local police well, and the local Marines (the only other authority in this remote area) he thought, as did I, that the bureaucracy in Mexico could sweep up poor little Peter and he could end up in an orphanage in Ensenada and be trapped there for months knowing the typical speed of governments.

I asked Peter about his grandparents to make sure he knew where to find them, and that he would want to go to them. He seemed relieved that this was the back-up plan to finding his father. He told me about fishing with his grandpa on the rivers of central California, and although I hate fishing and know little about it, I pretended to be very interested to keep his mind of other more pressing problems.

Meanwhile I was wondering how to get Peter back into the States. If we got stopped by Federales for passports (they still had drug roadblocks set up occasionally on the highway) we had no documentation for Peter. He didn't look anything like the Limey or me so it was unlikely we could claim he was either of ours. And neither of us looked old enough to have a kid that age. Perhaps I could claim he was my nephew and just be prepared to pay a large mordida, (a bribe that could fix almost anything in Baja.)

At the U.S. border they rarely asked for ID from Caucasians so I didn't anticipate a major problem. If there was, I would tell them the story and turn him over to the U.S. authorities. This was not my first choice, however, knowing how systems in any country tend to swallow people up. Peter seemed to trust me, and I would rather keep him with me until I could get him to his grandparents than turn him over to bureaucrats. I knew what I was planning could be seen as kidnapping, (and, if the father was pissed, would be) so my first move once in the U.S. would be to call the grandparents and set up a way to get him to them, ASAP.

Every once in a while, Miguel would curse under his breath in Spanish, wondering what kind of a sick cabrón could turn a child out into the desert to die. Miguel and I would discuss things in Spanish, but always in forced happy, upbeat tones in an attempt to not frighten Peter.

We got to Punta la Gringa asking everyone we saw, telling them if they saw the truck to send it to Tony's—everyone in the area knew the turtle research station.

We swung southward and cut cross-country to the road that leads into Bahia, the road on which Peter had been dumped. At the spot Peter said looked familiar, we stopped, and I even climbed up on top of the cab to look across the almost flat landscape to see...nothing. Just cacti and rocks.

We drove back to Tony's, got a negative report from the Limey, got some more water for the boy and dog (and us—it was hot out there), took a jug with us and set off again. We headed south now, into town, inquiring at the gas station and the three small stores where necessities including ice can be purchased, and the father might have stopped for supplies. No sign. We drove all along the beach, asking as we went, and again, no luck. How could he have disappeared? Miguel and I asked each other and wondered if indeed, the guy had abandoned the kid.

If he dropped the kid off, circled out through the desert and got back on the road, he would have easily covered the 60 km to the main road so it would be too late to set up a roadblock there. It would be hard to set up one on Route 1, but certainly the Mexican authorities could get the U.S. authorities to stop him when he tried to return to the U.S. But all of this might involve turning Peter over to the Mexican police—something Miguel and I agreed had to be avoided if at all possible.

Miguel said he could tell the local police that the guy had stolen something from him—they knew him well enough to believe him, and that could get the man stopped. But to what end I asked. If he really did intentionally leave this kid, there is no way in hell I am going to give Peter back to him. "But you would not see him punished for this crime?" Miguel said, adding, "I would see the bastard killed." If we could get the U.S. authorities to hold him on theft charges until I could get Peter safely to his grandparents then we could have the father charged with child abuse, and the U.S. authorities couldn't do anything to Miguel for filing a false police report about the alleged theft.

It was getting to be late afternoon, and Peter was getting nervous from all of our discussions in Spanish, so we started to talk about dinner and the big fiesta we had planned. Lots of food and fun with Miguel's kids. We had no such plans, but figured we didn't have much to give Peter to look forward to, so we planned a big dinner. We drove back through town and asked again at Diaz's store/gas station which is the focal point of the town. Still nothing, So we took one more swing out to the road where Peter had been left. Off in the distance, we saw a cloud of dust on the dirt road. We raced along to catch up to it and saw the red pick-up, minus the trailer. Miguel sped up to pass it and cut it off.

Miguel jumped out, grabbed the guy out of his truck, and slammed him up against the side of it. As I got out, the man looked at me, a fellow gringo, to appeal for help and asked what Miguel was screaming at him. The man didn't seem too excited to see Peter, not nearly as excited as a parent should be to see their possibly dead child come back to life.

Although Peter was thrilled to have found his father, he now seemed a little concerned that just as we found his dad, Miguel might kill him. I told the father that what Miguel was screaming at him was that he, too, was a father, and couldn't believe that any father could do such a stupid and cruel thing to a child.

I also wanted to kill the man, but tried to stay calm for Peter's sake. Then the man said to me, "Call off the wetback!" All I heard was the word "wetback" and for a second lost it and was lunging at the man until I heard Peter scream and I stopped. I looked at Peter's frightened face and realized Miguel and I were scaring the poor kid, and he had had enough trauma for one day. As much as his father deserved to die in that moment, Miguel and I couldn't be the ones to kill him. I stopped just short of hitting the father, but instead shook my fist in his face and told him in no uncertain terms that if he ever said anything like that again that I would help Miguel kill him, adding that "the wetback" probably saved his son's life.

I managed to get Miguel to let go of the man and I dragged the guy around the far side of the pickup so Peter couldn't hear what I was about to say, although as upset as I was, I'm sure he heard parts anyway. I yelled at him, (with more expletives than I am recording here), "Do you know anything about the desert?" He shook his head. "Do you know anything about dehydration?" He shook his head. "Do you know anything about exposure? Have you ever been to Mexico before? Ever been to the desert before? Do you know anything about rattlesnakes or scorpions or anything about anything, you stupid son of a bitch and sorry excuse for a human being, let alone father..." He shook his head, some of this starting to sink in, whether out of fear of me, or comprehension, I don't know. Although he was much bigger than me, I don't think either of us doubted that I was pissed off enough to kill him. "To do that to a dog is sick and inhumane, but to do that to a child! Your own child!"

He said he meant to just scare the kid, and come right back, but got lost, then found where he decided to camp, so went ahead and camped, figuring the kid would be okay for a couple hours out there — what trouble could he get into? Then he drove around a while until he thought he found the right road. I asked when he had dropped Peter off. That had been 10 a.m. Peter had come to me a little after 2 and it was now after 6. I asked if he would leave his kid alone in a shopping mall in the U.S. for eight hours. He still didn't seem 100 percent convinced that he had done something very wrong.

I grabbed him by the shirt, leaned in close and assured him that if he ever did anything like that again that Miguel and I would track him down and kill him. I think he believed me. I told him to wait; I wanted to talk to Peter. I walked back around to where Peter was and squatted down next to him. I told him he knew where I was camped and where Miguel lived and was a smart kid and could find his way back there, and that if needed us, to come find us. That the offer to take him back to the States and his grandpa still was available. I asked him a couple times if he really wanted to go with his father.

He said his father wasn't really a bad person; he just got angry and did stupid things. Peter said, "I shouldn't have gotten him mad." I hugged Peter and told him that whatever he did, this was NOT his fault and he didn't do anything to deserve to be scared like this.

But father and son were reunited and they drove off. Miguel drove me back to my beach- front palapa; we were shaking our heads and saying little. The Limey was anxious to hear that we found Peter's father. Miguel dropped me off and drove home to report back to his wife.

I told the Limey I felt bad about leaving her, and an amazing thing happened. I saw her fall in love with me. It is the only time in my life that I have witnessed that moment. I have known other people have loved me, but she and I had not been dating that long, and I knew she liked me, but at that moment, it turned from like to love. She threw her arms around me and kissed me and told me that she wouldn't have thought much of me if I hadn't done everything I could to help Peter.

A couple of days later, she and I went for a long walk down the beach and we saw Peter out playing on the sand. He seemed happy collecting shells. I looked around and saw his father about 100 yards away from the water, cleaning fish. He looked up saw me and went back to his work. Before I could ask, Peter quickly said everything was fine, and again apologized for his father. He said again his father just lost his temper now and then but wasn't a bad person. It was so sad that at age 10, this kid has already learned to cover for his father. Parental rights being what they are, I knew that there was no way to interfere. I have never wanted kids and don't particularly like kids, but at that moment I would have adopted Peter and I'm sure I'd have been a better parent than the one he had.

I always think of that line from *Parenthood* where Keanu Reeve's character says, "You need a license to own a dog, you need a license to catch a fish, but they will let any asshole be a parent."

I hope Peter is well.

Dangers on the Road

WE heard a shot. All three of our spines went rigid against the seat of the pickup truck. My friend said, "We're not going back." Our other friend added, "Oh hell no."

I chimed in, "Whatever just happened, we don't want to know about and can't change it anyway." I was tempted to speed up, but if those Federales were paying any attention to us, I thought it might seem suspicious. Even though my heart was pounding and I was concerned about breaking the steering wheel from gripping it so tightly, I kept my eyes fixed on the road and kept driving a steady speed with unsteady hands.

As the drug war that straddled the U.S.-Mexico border got worse, visits to Baja got scarier and the incident in which a Mexican farmer may have been killed was one of several that had me too frightened to go down there; about 1994 I stopped making the trips. Also, the magazine about Baja for which I had been freelancing went out of business and I was finding it much harder to sell articles to pay for my vacations.

I am eager to go back to Baja someday and see how much has changed and how much has stayed the same.

On our last few trips, we encountered roadblocks all along Mexican Federal Highway 1, the only road that goes the entire length of the Baja peninsula from Tijuana to Cabo San Lucas. Each checkpoint had a vehicle, often an Army truck, blocking one of the lanes; the other lane sometimes had a barrier like the ones that are seen at road construction projects or the parking lots of football stadiums—two wooden A-frames holding a crossbar.

Most of these roadblocks were staffed the same. There would be eight or 12 very young-looking soldiers in ill-fitting camouflage, like they were 15-year-olds wearing their older brothers' army uniforms. They each carried an automatic rifle in a battle-ready stance, but held the gun in the way that I might if someone handed me an oversized weapon that was loaded, the safety was off, and I had no idea where the trigger was. The officer in command was the only one who looked old enough to shave or vote. He invariably was not in uniform at all, but rather wore blue jeans, a Hawaiian shirt, and had an automatic pistol shoved down the front of his belt. I wondered if the government wanted the officers to dress this way to add an element of casual threat to the encounter. I wasn't sure of whom to be more afraid—the kids who clearly didn't know how to use their guns or the officer who clearly did and probably had.

There was something so irregular about the operation, we wondered that if the soldiers killed us all, buried our bodies in the desert, and stole our truck and all our gear would they even have to fill out any paperwork? Or was that just routine collateral damage of drug interdiction?

On our last trips we'd encounter four or six such roadblocks and after a while we never made a trip in which we didn't encounter at least one stop. The process was always a bit scary. Sometimes the officer would casually ask, in English, "Do you have any guns? Drugs? Marijuana? Pistols?" I wondered if they ever caught anyone this way. If the driver cracked and confessed, "Yes, okay, fine, you got me! I have three keys of cocaine and an AK-47!" We always answered in the negative. Most of the time that was the end of it and we were allowed to drive on.

Other times the officer or his boys would search the vehicle. Sometimes it was just a cursory search, barely lifting or moving anything. Other times they wanted us to take everything out of the truck, then they'd rummage through it and leave us to repack all the gear. Between the search and reassembly, it could sometimes take an hour or two.

One time when we opened the truck's camper shell for the officer, his eyes immediately rested on the cooler. He asked, in Spanish, "What is in here?" I answered, "Cerveza." His eyes lit up. "Fria?" he asked. I opened the cooler to show him that we indeed had cold beer on ice. He started to reach for one so I quickly asked if he would like one, commenting that it was a hot day and he might need one. He smiled. I pulled out two bottles and handed them to him. I suggested he might want some for his men. He said, no, just one more for him. I obliged. Nice to know he didn't want to get too drunk on the job. That was the end of his search. It was the cheapest mordida I ever had to bribe a Federale with. Definitely worth three beers to get moving again.

Then there was the shooting. I was taking my turn behind the wheel. I saw the roadblock and was slowing down. Parked on the shoulder of the road was a beat-up old pickup truck which had an even more dilapidated trailer hitched to it. The Mexican officer in the standard Hawaiian shirt was yelling at the driver of the pickup. He paused his harangue to motion for me to pull up and stop even with the pickup. I complied. I watched as he screamed a few more Spanish obscenities at the ancient man behind the wheel of the pickup. The old man returned a few choice words. Not things I would yell at an angry army officer who had a gun and was backed up by his dozen youngsters with even bigger guns. The officer ordered the old man to stay put.

Then the officer walked around our truck and to my driver's window. He asked some of the routine questions. Where were we going? Why? For how long? Did we have any illegal…as I was about to answer another question the officer whipped out his pistol and shoved it into the cab of our pickup. He was pointing it through our truck at the old farmer who had just restarted his truck.

The ancient truck sputtered and coughed and backfired so if the ancient man thought he was going to sneak away, that was not happening. The officer was screaming in Spanish to turn off the fucking truck right now! The officer had the pistol right in front of my face. His trigger finger was about six inches in front of my nose. I closed my eyes. I was worried that if he pulled the trigger, my eyes would get scorched by the flash of gunpowder. I tried to flatten myself back into the headrest as far as I could go as I listened to the guy with the pistol screaming at the old man. To my shock, the farmer was yelling back, equally foul and angry words. My Spanish isn't good enough to catch everything they were saying, but the farmer was angry that he was being detained so long and wanted to get about his business. The guy with the gun was adamant that he could keep him there all fucking day if he wanted! Or did he want them to strip the truck? Did he want to go to jail?

The yelling and the tension were rising. I hoped it wouldn't be capped with a gunshot when suddenly the officer stopped yelling mid-sentence. I cracked an eye open to what had stopped him. He was looking at me as though he was seeing me for the first time. He switched from angry Spanish to bland, bureaucratic English and said to me, "Oh, I'm sorry. You can go." He retracted the gun from the cab, took a step back and made a polite gesture with his arm that I could pass, like a maître d' showing us to our table. The shift of mood and tone was beyond jarring and although I was very glad to be driving on, it was startling and frightening. Out of the corner of my eye, I saw the farmer's truck start to pull forward and immediately the officer resumed yelling. The old truck was pulling out quite slowly, whether again he thought the military man wouldn't notice or that was all the faster the old thing would move, I don't know.

We were only about 100 yards down the road when we heard the shot.

There was no way we were going back to see what happened.

Crazy things were happening more frequently. On one trip to Bahia de Los Angeles, we saw the hulk of an airplane in the desert about halfway between the road and the airport. It was a newish plane, possibly an eight-seater Piper or Cessna. It hadn't been there on our last visit. We asked how it got there and one of our Mexican friends told us that it had made a forced landing. It must have had some sort of engine trouble and tried to land at the airport, but couldn't quite make it and set down in the desert instead.

When the authorities pulled up, whoever was on board was gone. No trace of people. What was on board were dozens of bricks of cocaine. Probably millions of dollars' worth of the stuff. The Mexican officials took all of the drugs. Whether to turn in to higher authority or to resell themselves, no one around there was dumb enough to ask. After narcotics officials left the area, the plane sat for a week or so. The locals were afraid to go near it for fear the people who owned those drugs would be back. But after it became apparent no one was coming for the goods, the neighbors stripped the plane of its engine, radios, seats, and anything else of any value. No sense letting it rot in the desert as so many old cars did in the area. They figured if the plane's owners hadn't come back in a short while, they weren't going to, probably fearing the authorities would be waiting to arrest them. And after a few days, clearly there'd be no point in coming back.

The drugs would surely have been taken and the plane wasn't worth nearly as much as the coke, and certainly not worth the risk of coming back to try to fix it and fly it out. The plane made the locals nervous and acutely more aware that the dangers of the drug wars were getting closer and closer to home. If you saw the wrong thing, the cartels wouldn't hesitate to kill you, or you could get caught in the crossfire between warring factions and the authorities, either from Mexico or the U.S. I couldn't help but wonder what happens to a pilot and crew who goes to tell their boss that they sort of lost his plane full of drugs. I doubt that part of the story had a pleasant outcome.

One final incident that made up our minds that it was no longer safe to go to Baja, was one that involved no visible firearms or shootings or drugs, but was weirdly intimidating. I was driving my Isuzu Rodeo up a dry stream bed when we saw a Jeep Cherokee with California plates coming at us. The stream bed was soft sand and I know from experience that if I stopped in soft sand, it might be tough to get moving again without spinning the wheels. I also knew how bad Cherokees are in sand. I had used my Rodeo to tow a few of them off beaches and from other places where they got stuck. I looked for a flat place where I could pull out of the sandy stream bed onto solid ground to let the Jeep pass. I found one and rode up onto the dirt.

The Cherokee came alongside and, as was usual when you encountered folks in the middle of nowhere, they stopped. It was custom to exchange pleasantries. This exchange was more frightening than pleasant. My two friends and I got out of my car. Three guys got out of the Cherokee. They were all wearing dress pants, white button-down dress shirts, dress shoes, and blue windbreakers, even though it was very hot in the desert. My friends and I were in tank tops and shorts. And the three Americans opposite us were wearing mirrored aviator sunglasses. Already this was creepy.

One of the guys in the windbreakers asked, as though he was a police officer questioning a witness, "What are you guys doing out here?"

One of my friends answered that we had heard about some interesting rock paintings and wanted to see them. He asked the starched shirts if they knew where they were or had been there. They shook their heads. My friend asked what they were doing out there. One of the mysterious men answered, "Fishing." We were many miles from

Some of the many Native rock paintings we sought out in Baja.

water on either side of the peninsula. There was no water in the stream. There was no access from this stream bed to open water. And these guys were about as properly dressed to go fishing as I was to visit the moon. It would have been like asking a guy making a pizza what he was doing and without the slightest hint of sarcasm or humor, him answering, "Brain surgery" as though that should have been obvious from the way he was conducting himself.

They asked where we were from. We answered, "Los Angeles." We asked where they were from and they answered, vaguely, "The United States."

Without making it too obvious, I tried to see if they had guns under their windbreakers. And wondered if they were DEA, FBI, customs officials or who they were. One thing I knew for sure: they were not sport fishermen. Their other questions and answers were equally disturbing. As with the roadblocks run by the Mexican government, I wondered if these men, who clearly worked for the U.S. government in some capacity, killed us and left our bodies for the vultures, would they have to fill out any paperwork on the incident? Was there even a form to fill out for incidents like this? Or would we just be unknown casualties of the drug war? No one knew where we were or to come looking for us.

Without even discussing that we should. my friends and I started moving toward the Rodeo and opening the doors, saying with forced politeness, "Guess we should be going…"

The men said perfunctory goodbyes and got in their Jeep. The guy hit the gas too hard and the Jeep started spinning in the sand. For a moment, I was worried he was going to spin the tires in and dig a hole for himself. I had a tow rope and knew I could pull him out, but I didn't want to spend one more minute with these guys than we had to. The guy in the passenger seat seemed to talk him into taking his foot off the gas and trying to pull out much more slowly. They drove off.

We headed further upstream in search of the rock paintings, but all of us were sweating and nervous, not sure what there was to fear, but knowing we wanted to give those guys wide berth.

Clueless Travelers . . .
Over the years, I Have Encountered a Few

IT has been my experience that many people seem to give their brains a vacation while they are traveling. A few examples.

I was teaching traffic school at a motel, not far from the beach in Carlsbad, California one evening. While waiting for class to start, I was talking to the desk clerk who I had gotten to know from having taught there so often. A motel guest came up to the desk and apologized for interrupting our conversation, then asked the clerk where and what time he and his family could get a bus to the caverns in the morning.

The clerk politely asked, "You mean Carlsbad Caverns?" The man said, of course. The clerk again, very politely said, "Sir, those are in New Mexico." The man asked what he meant. The clerk calmly and professionally explained that there was a Carlsbad, New Mexico and a Carlsbad, California. The caverns were in the Carlsbad in New Mexico. There were no caverns in this Carlsbad. Just a beach. The man flew into a rage. What the hell do you mean there are no caverns here? We booked this vacation specifically to see the caverns! Why did no one warn us when we booked this trip that this Carlsbad is in the wrong state?" The clerk tried to explain that there are lots of people who come to the Carlsbad in California for lots of reasons, and they can't guess who might be looking for caverns in the wrong state.

The man wanted a refund! The motel had booked the room under false pretenses! He kept ranting as I had to walk away from the desk and go teach my class. At the break in class, I went back to the clerk and asked him if this happened often and he nodded. "At least once a week, all summer long. About once a month in the winter." He said people had suggested that they start answering the phones, "The ___ Motel.

There are no caverns anywhere near here." He said he told the guy to talk to the manager in the morning, but he wouldn't be getting a refund. I mean, if you are dumb enough to book a hotel in the wrong state, 1000 miles away from the caverns...

I could sympathize with the poor clerk. When I worked at the motel in Venice, we regularly had guests ask, "Why is the ocean so far from the motel?" I wasn't sure how to answer that. "Because God put the ocean too far away?" "Wait for a big earthquake, it will move closer." Of course the motel frowned on us being smartasses to the guests so I would just try to calmly explain it was a mile away. I don't know why they thought it was closer. The descriptions in the AAA book and other travel guides all said it was a mile to the beach. Pointing that out did not make the guests any happier.

Then there was the evening I was working at the motel in Venice and a couple from Japan asked me to call them a cab. I picked up the phone to dial and said, "Of course. Where to?" They said, "San Francisco." I put the phone back down. I said, "I can't do that." They asked why not. They wanted to have dinner there. (It was now about 6 p.m.) I told them they wouldn't get there until after midnight and I doubted any cab driver would take that fare. It was over 400 miles.

They argued with me that it was closer than that and they insisted I call them a cab. I told them I could, but I didn't think a cab was the best way to go. The man pulled out a map of California that fit on a standard-sized sheet of printer paper and showed me how close Los Angeles was to San Francisco. About two inches. Not far at all.

I again tried to explain how big California was and that his map didn't accurately represent that. He was getting more and more angry and demanded I call a cab. I said I would, but he should ask the driver how much the fare would be before he got in the cab. I watched from the lobby as the man yelled "What?" at the cab driver who had apparently told him the bad news I had tried to convey. The man and his wife walked out of the parking lot and presumably to a restaurant that was a little closer.

Sometimes the clueless people in hotels were the ones behind the registration desks. I would occasionally have to teach traffic school at the Hilton Hotel in Sherman Oaks. And I hated it for a stupid reason: the clocks above their front desk. Like many hotels, they tried to appear more international by having clocks representing major cities around the world. I tried to explain to each desk clerk I met that their clocks were wrong. Each clerk had the same answer, "That's because they represent the times in different time zones." And I could never get it through to them that if it's 8:13 in Los Angeles, it can't be 11:47 in New York and 5:32 in London and 11:21 in Shanghai. I tried and tried to explain that yes, although the hours are different from place to place, it is 13 minutes past the hour everywhere! They never got it and never changed their clocks. I hope no one planned any business calls based on their time zones.

We're Not in Kansas...
and Other Drives Across the U.S.

And Why Do They Have One of
Douglas MacArthur's Spurs?
And Other Stories...

IF I don't know about something, I want to learn. Sometimes that can be hard to do as I discovered at a museum in a small town in Kansas. On my first drive across the United States, as much as practical and possible, I tried to stay off the interstates. Iowa looks pretty much the same as Maine from the highway. Get onto the alternate routes, what William Least Heat-Moon called the *Blue Highways*, and there is no way to mistake New England for the Midwest.

I always tried to opt for the local diner rather than a chain or fast-food restaurant. I wanted to soak up the atmosphere, hear the chatter, and see what the local scene had to offer. I learned that almost every town had some little factoid of which they were proud. Often they had a small, quaint museum dedicated to the town's history and the one or two quasi-famous people who came from that town. Pretty much every one of those museums in the Midwest has a taxidermied jackalope. You have not really seen America until you have seen a stuffed and mounted jackalope. Just pray you never see a live one in the wild. They are dangerous creatures.

In a little hamlet in Kansas, the clerk at the gas station, the waitress and the person running the register at the café—almost everyone I encountered—boasted of the town's claim to fame. Apparently they didn't get a lot of visitors. Most travelers stuck to I-70 which ran about 50 miles north. I was obviously an outsider even if they hadn't seen the Pennsylvania license plates. They all asked some version of, "Have you visited our museum? We have one of Douglas MacArthur's spurs." After four or five people had promoted that unlikely tourist attraction,

I felt the obligation to check it out. I was taking the scenic route across America to see things, and after all, how often do you get to visit one of Douglas MacArthur's spurs?

I paid the nominal admission fee at the museum, and there, centered in the building's one large room, was a square glass case. Under the glass were several well-positioned lights illuminating a white silk cloth and there, beautifully displayed in the middle of the case was a spur. One polished silver spur. I studied it for a moment. Then I looked around the case for some sort of little title card that would tell me the provenance of this unusual object. There was none.

I turned to the woman behind the counter to whom I had paid my admission and said, "So this spur belonged to Douglas MacArthur?"

Her face lit up brighter than the white silk in the case. Clearly she did not get many visitors who took an interest in their prize possession. "That's right," she beamed. "That spur belonged to General Douglas MacArthur!"

I was curious. I had to know more. "Where is the other spur?" I asked, knowing enough about horsemanship to be aware that these things tended to come in pairs.

Her smile faded just a little. Apparently she had not been asked that before. "I don't know," she answered. It was not an answer I expected, but I still had so much to learn.

"Was Douglas MacArthur ever in the cavalry that he needed spurs?" (At the point in my life, all I knew about Doug was his World War II service.)

Losing a little more of her smile, she replied, "Oh, I don't know."

I pressed on. "Did Douglas MacArthur live in this town at some point?"

Her smile was completely gone. "Oh…I don't know."

"Was he stationed near here?"

Her smile was now a frown. Clearly she was not prepared for a quiz. "I don't know."

"How did his spur end up in this town?"

Her answer came back a little quieter, like a schoolgirl called to the front of class by the teacher to prove she had not done her reading. "I don't know."

"How did the museum come by the spur?"

Defeated, she sighed, "I don't know."

I regretted that I had made her feel bad so I thought I would soften the blow by offering her a plausible excuse for knowing nothing about the town's most prized artifact. "I understand. Are you just a volunteer here at the museum?

"Oh no," she said proudly, her smile returning. "I'm the museum's curator!"

I dutifully checked out their jackalope then hit the trail out of town, headed to Dodge.

But before Dodge, I had to hit another tourist attraction that came highly recommended. This one did not disappoint. *The Garden of Eden* in Lucas, Kansas has to be in my top 10 for most bizarre cultural hotspots.

If you're ever in Kansas, The Garden of Eden is one of the strangest tourist attractions I've ever visited and worth the side trip to Lucas.

In the early 1900s, an elderly Civil War veteran named Samuel Dinsmoor decided to reconstruct the Garden of Eden out of reinforced concrete as social commentary. His skills as a sculptor were somewhat lacking and the Adam and Eve figures look like a 4-year-old might make out of Play-Doh. He then went on to build a concrete log cabin. He built a log-shaped mold into which to pour concrete and created massive, heavy "logs" out of which he built his house.

By the time he did all of this, he was rather old and knew his time was coming so he built a mausoleum on the property and in it made a concrete coffin with a glass lid. He had stipulated that it should cost 10 cents to tour the Garden of Eden and the concrete log cabin house and for five cents you could go into the mausoleum and see Mr. Dinsmoor decomposing under glass. After you've driven 50 miles out of your way and spent the dime, you kinda have to go the extra nickel and go into the mausoleum. And sure enough, there he was. Not as gruesome as I would have expected.

I checked the Garden's website and although they have raised the admission prices, Eden and Mr. Dinsmoor are still there. I was surprised years later when I was reading the book *In Awe* by Scott Heim and there was a crucial scene set in the Garden of Eden. Scott and I have since become friends and yes, Scott is from Kansas.

In my travels, I learned that there are dozens of towns across the U.S. that claim to have the world's smallest church or the world's smallest post office or the world's smallest something. Or the world's largest ball of twine.

And I learned something else: if anything claims to be "The World Famous..." it's not. Find me one person in China who has ever heard of "The World Famous Garden of Eden" or five people outside of Kansas who have ever heard of "The World Famous Garden of Eden." There are "World Famous" balls of twine and "World Famous" mystery spots and "World Famous" diners and again I challenge you to find anyone from even two counties over who ever heard of them.

My theory is that if something is really "World Famous" they do not need a sign that says that. There is no sign in front of the Taj Mahal that says, "The World Famous Taj Mahal!" You knew that. That is pretty much the reason you went to Agra, India. There are no signs that say "The World Famous Eiffel Tower" or "The World Famous Great Wall of China." They don't need to tell you it's world famous if it really is. Just an observation. But of course, even though no more than the 100 people who live within spitting distance of a tourist attraction have ever heard of it, doesn't mean I won't stop and check it out. After all, how else would I have seen one of Douglas MacArthur's spurs?

The other quirky spot in Kansas was Salina, in the center of the state. Locals liked to refer to Salina as "The Home of the Space Shuttle." Apparently a leftover World War II bomber strip was one of the longest runways in the United States and was designated as something like the fourth back-up emergency landing site for the Space Shuttle. Their 2.5 miles of concrete was long enough for a Shuttle landing and apparently every time the shuttle was up, a crew would inspect the runway and make sure emergency vehicles and other equipment were ready, just in case.

Like Douglas MacArthur's spur this was the town's only claim to fame and they were milking it for all it was worth. I could just imagine that every time the Space Shuttle took off the Salina City Council and Chamber of Commerce would hold vigils, praying there would be bad weather at the Cape in Florida, Edwards Air Force Base in California, and that airbase in Texas so that once, just once, the Shuttle would have to land in Salina and call national attention to their city. Of course, the Shuttle was retired without that ever happening. Poor Salina.

A place worth seeing was Dwight Eisenhower's boyhood home in Abilene. They have a small, well-done museum of his childhood, military leadership including his key role in winning World War II, and his time as president. Given my interest in history and my later visit to the museums in France pertaining to D-Day, I did enjoy this visit.

My other stop in Kansas was Hays. A coworker of my father's was Alexander Hays IV. The town was named after Fort Hays, which had been named after General Alexander Hays. (*see: Six Degrees of Gettysburg in Section VI.*) Alex said that years earlier the Hays family had loaned some of the general's artifacts to the university to display in the library and he was wondering how they were doing. Always up for a new destination, and since Hays was just off I-70, I agreed to stop in and was happy to report that the general's sword was still nicely exhibited in the library. What I found most interesting was that there was a herd of buffalo grazing on the campus. How Kansas is that?

I thought it was interesting that the Hays family had a town named for them, and frankly, I was a bit jealous. Earlier in this cross-country adventure, I had visited the town of Meyer, Iowa and drove away very let down. At the time, I thought there was only one town in the U.S. named Meyer. I have since learned of two others. I drove out of my way in Iowa to visit Meyer, although as far as I know it has no connection to my family. I was disappointed to see it was a crossroads. That was it. Two county or state routes intersecting and a sign proclaiming it to be Meyer. There was a barn a few hundred yards from the intersection, but driving down each of the roads a mile or two revealed no other signs of human habitation. No houses, no store, no church, no cemetery. Just the sign and the barn. Hardly worth the drive. But such is the luck of random drives across America.

In Kansas, I also saw my first tornado. It was way off in the distance, the black funnel cloud. It was fascinating and scary at once. I wanted to get closer, but I didn't want it to get too close. I dialed around the radio to find a local station to keep track of it. It veered north, away from me as I drove west.

The closest I came to a tornado was in northern Mississippi a few years later, driving east across the country with a friend. We had a little rain and wind as we were driving through the countryside in the late afternoon, but didn't think much of it until we finally hit a town. We had been looking for a place to eat for hours. We were well past dinnertime and hungry. All of the power was out. We drove the length of town on its main street, at times having to steer around downed power lines and tree limbs and pieces of storefronts and signs and roofs. Every building was dark. Traffic signals were out and some were dangling dangerously from broken poles and damaged wires. All the restaurants were dark.

I had never seen the immediate aftermath of a tornado, but this was clearly it. We skirted the debris in the road. We got through the business district and were abandoning hope of finding anyplace open for dinner when we noticed the lights on in a Pizza Hut. We slowed down and saw it had customers inside so we pulled in. When we placed our order, we learned they did indeed have a twister that afternoon. The Pizza Hut had its own generator and was able to reopen quickly once the storm passed. No one was killed or seriously hurt, and the damage, by local tornado standards, was not that bad.

The table next to ours was occupied by about six teenagers who, from the tone of their conversation, were apparently the local high school's cool-kid clique. They were comparing stories on what they had found when they all-clear was sounded and they emerged from the school's basement and dashed home. Most found a few broken windows and downed tree branches, but minimal destruction, considering.

The one boy, clearly a jock, said in his thick southern accent that he first ran to his father's store to check on his Dad and the business since it was closer. His father was fine and was sweeping up broken glass from the shattered windows. The Dad said he'd been trying to call home, but the phone lines were down. He said he'd stay there and board up the windows and gave his son his car keys, telling him to go home and check on the mother.

In that accent dripping of magnolia blossoms, the teen described how when he got home the front window was gone and the front door was off its hinges. Now he was very worried about his mother and went room to room calling out, "Mama! Are you all right, Mama?" He got to the bathroom and the door was closed. He hollered again for his mother as he opened the door. There was a mattress covering the tub and peeking out between the mattress and the tub rim was the business end of a double-barrel shotgun. He said, "Lordy, Mama, don't shoot! It's me, your only son, Craig! Put that damn gun down or you'll never have grandchildren!"

He helped his mother clean up the house, reported back to his father, then met his friends.

Note to self: when driving cross-country, check the local radio stations occasionally for storm warnings.

Barely Greeting the Sunrise

ON my first drive to California, I had a plan, but deviated from it at times either because of new opportunities or poor planning. For instance, I had intended to camp at the Grand Canyon not realizing those campgrounds would be full in mid-August. My next stop was Las Vegas so I began working my way in that direction. Most of the campgrounds I encountered had their "No Vacancy" signs out. I didn't want to spend what little money I had on a motel knowing I'd likely have to spring for one in Sin City.

Finally, at Marble Canyon, Arizona, I found a spot. It was a lovely canyon, with interesting rock formations at least what I could see

Light from the rising sun illuminating the rocks in Marble Canyon, Arizona.

of them in the fading light. As I was pitching my tent, the handsome man in the next camping spot came over and said hello. He spoke only broken English. He was a student from Japan and was spending the summer seeing some of the U.S. before returning home in a few weeks to continue his studies. Like me, he had hopes of camping at the Grand Canyon, but this was as close as he could get.

(Side note about the Grand Canyon. No matter how many descriptions you have read, no matter how many photos or videos you have seen, you have not experienced one percent of the awe you feel standing on the rim. There are no words or pixels that can come close to the real deal. At this point, I am at a loss to write more because I would just be reciting the same old clichés like "breathtaking." It is so much more than that.)

My campground neighbor and I had a nice visit, but since it was dark and we lacked lights or alcohol, there wasn't much to do but say goodnight. It was a primitive campground with no store or amenities, just some spaces marked in the dirt and a community bathroom. We were both tired and crawled into our tents.

A few hours later, I heard something. Once I was awake, I realized it was my neighbor. He said he was very sorry to wake me, but he thought I might want to see something. I peeked out of the tent flap and he pointed up at the sky. The heavens were alive with meteors. It was the Perseids meteor shower completely unencumbered by any surrounding man-made lights and the firmament was the 4th of July writ large. I kept my eyes fixed on the show as I climbed out of my tent to stand with my new friend and enjoy the wonders of nature.

I had seen a few shooting stars the previous night while I was camped in Utah, but had not stayed up late enough to catch the bulk of show. Now I was enjoying the sky show of a lifetime. Shooting stars of various sizes and intensities, one after another. My new friend and I stood there for hours quietly talking, but mainly just enjoying the spectacle in silence. Again, words such as "awe" are so inadequate. This many decades later, I can still feel the way my blood flowed with fire watching it.

As the sun started coming up, its growing light made the heavenly extravaganza harder to see. I had no idea how long we had been frozen in time, just the student and I having the sky to ourselves. We agreed the best of the show was pretty much over and he said to me, "You may want to put some clothes on before the rest of the camp gets up." I looked down. I had been standing there naked the whole time. It was quite warm when I got in my tent, so I had stripped down and was sleeping on top of my sleeping bag with nothing on. From the moment I looked out the tent flap I had been so mesmerized by the stars that I hadn't given a moment's thought to what I was or wasn't wearing.

I reached into my tent, pulled out my shorts and put them on. He and I agreed there would be no point trying to go back to bed for another hour or two. We were both too high on nature to be able to sleep. The sun was rising, and the day and new adventures beckoned. The dawn was glorious, in part due to the afterglow of a night spent in something more enriching than sleep. And the rocks around the canyon glowed red, as though made of stained glass and backlit from within the earth.

The student and I quietly chatted as we packed our gear and struck our tents. We should have hugged goodbye. We shared a moment and a bond that was too special for a simple handshake, but that is all we did to say farewell. He was heading north to the National Parks of Utah where I had just been. I was heading west to Las Vegas.

I made some stops along the way and it was late when I hit the Vegas. I was driving down the Strip for the first time in my life, marveling at the neon all around me. Spectacular even then though the casinos were, they were nothing compared to what they are today. Suddenly the sky lit up and traffic stopped. People on the sidewalks froze. A light a million times brighter than all the lights on the Strip illuminated the sky. A giant meteor with a power and glow that seemed capable of ending life on the planet burst through the heavens. It put all the puny electric bulbs of men to shame. Jaded as Las Vegas gamblers may be, I could hear people ohhhhing and awwwwing all around me. I still have never seen a meteor that rivaled the one that welcomed me to Las Vegas. It was a few moments until everyone collected themselves and life on earth slowly resumed.

I found a cheap casino with cheap rooms and for the first time in my life I tried real gambling on their rather dirty, and very smoky, gambling floor. I was nervous about risking $10 in a video poker machine, but I didn't know when I'd be back to Las Vegas and had to at least try it. Only a few hands in, I won $125. More than enough to cover my hotel and the breakfast buffet before leaving in the morning. I guess I could have afforded one of the cheap motels in the middle-of-nowhere Arizona, north of the Grand Canyon. But if I had, I would have missed one of the most amazing nights of my life, watching meteors with the young man from Japan.

More Adventures on the Road . . .

I was driving back from a trip to Humboldt, California. I was taking back roads as much as possible and was tired after not getting much sleep for a few days. I was eager to get to San Francisco and to the apartment of the friends with whom I'd be staying the night. I stopped for gas somewhere north of San Francisco. By the time I got gas, a snack, used the bathroom, and relaxed for a minute, I guess my tiredness took its toll and I sort of lost track of where I was. I went back inside the gas station/convenience store and up to the woman at the counter. Pointing down the road, I asked her, "How far is it to San Francisco down this way?" She considered for only a moment and then replied, "That way? That way, San Francisco is about 24 or 25,000 miles." She clearly enjoyed my puzzled look and then, pointing the opposite direction said, "San Francisco is about 40 miles that way. If you go the way you were pointing, it's going to take you a while." I had to laugh. And was impressed she knew the approximate circumference of the Earth.

When I first moved to Los Angeles, I used to visit a friend in San Luis Obispo and would drive different routes to see more of California and make the drives more interesting. It was on one of those alternate routes that I encountered the town New Cuyama. And I had to stop

I had to love a little town like New Cuyama with a goofy sense of humor.

and take a photo of their sign. Clever way to get people to remember their little hamlet.

I always enjoyed it when I got within range of the Santa Maria radio station. They did radio versions of spoof ads of the sort for which *Saturday Night Live* was famous. They sounded so real and they mixed them in with real ads for fertilizer and tractors, so that it often took a moment to catch that it was a joke. One I recall was a public service announcement in which a man's deep, authoritative voice said something like, "Hello, my name is Dr. Leonard Spencer. When I was a boy, my mother used to say, 'Lenny, put down that pointy stick. You'll poke someone's eye out.' But now that I am a doctor, I have never seen anyone's eye poked out with a pointy stick. And I have learned that pointy sticks are important for lots of things, like staking up tomato plants and making shish kabobs. It just goes to show you mom didn't know everything." And then a woman's voice came on and said, "This has been a public service announcement from the National Council for Sharp Pointy Sticks. For more information write, 'Pointy Stick, Washington, DC, 20024.'"

An equally deadpan joke I enjoyed so much I still remember it, was when I was touring Hearst Castle, the fabulous estate of William Randolph Heart in San Simeon that was the inspiration for Xanadu in Orson Welles' *Citizen Kane*. The tour guide calmly intoned the facts and figures of many of the works of art we passed. "Notice the tapestry on the east wall. It was purchased by Mr. Hearst in Spain for $1.2 million dollars in 1926." And as we were about to leave one room he said, "As we enter this next room, I want you to pay special attention to the plastic floor runner. It was purchased from Sears, Roebuck and Company in Santa Barbara in 1977 for $15.99." He waited until we all registered our confusion as to why he was including this as being of significance to add, with absolutely no betrayal of emotion or humor, "It will be quite memorable to you if you step off it onto the priceless silk French rug, because you will be rushed off the premises so fast it'll make your head spin."

On one of the tips I took across the U.S., my friend and I decided to drive late into the night to make the next town. Suddenly out of the sky came bright lights. They flew low and fast, coming right at us. As tired as we were, we were sure we were about to be abducted by aliens. The unidentified flying object raced toward us at high speed about 30 feet off the ground. We wondered if it was just going to scoop up the car or if a tractor beam would remove us from the car a la *Star Trek*'s transporters or however it is that Martians seize subjects for their experiments?

It passed directly above us; the lights were so bright we couldn't even make out its size and shape. Before our blinded eyes could even adjust to the darkness, it left in its wake. It made an impossibly fast turn and zipped back at us, leaving our eyes useless in the white lights. We didn't know if we should slow down because we couldn't see the road or try to speed away before it returned, but before we could choose a course of action, it was on us again, blinding us. It made pass after pass, barely clearing the car. It was taking turns and making maneuvers no normal human plane could execute. Perhaps they were deciding if it should collect one or both specimens from the car. We could no longer see to drive, and had to stop to await our fate. Then it flew farther than it had in any previous pass and as our vision came back, we were able to see it make its turn. It was just an ultralight being used as a crop duster.

On my cross-country drives, I always make it a priority to visit the homes of writers, presidents, and other notables. I have been to John Steinbeck's house, and Ernest Hemingway's house. I have been to Walden Pond. I have been to several of Mark Twain's houses,

The tiny cabin Mark Twain shared with his fellow writer Bret Harte in the Gold Country of California.

including his boyhood home in Hannibal, Missouri and the cabin he shared with Bret Harte in the California Gold Country. His home in Hartford, Connecticut stands next to that of another famous author, Harriet Beecher Stowe. I visited both. Neither of the writers were at home. I guess I should have called first. I have been to the homes of Eisenhower, Grant, Harding, Buchanan, FDR, Hoover, and other presidents. In addition to hoping to pick up some good writing vibes, I always like to learn a little history along the way.

When I first got my four-wheel drive, I liked to sort of test its limits, sometimes with mixed results. When a college buddy came out to Southern California to go with me to the Rose Bowl to see Penn

My college buddy trying to shovel enough snow out from under my Isuzu Rodeo to get us moving again.

State play, we wanted to go exploring and headed to the backside of the Sierras off Route 395 near Death Valley. I managed to get the Isuzu Rodeo high-centered on snow. We were many miles from the nearest pay phone, on an untraveled side road. Help would not be coming. We'd have to get ourselves out. Our only tool for digging was my emergency Frisbee. With our cold hands and a poor excuse for a shovel, it took hours to free the vehicle and get on our way, something my friend teases me about to this day.

That emergency Frisbee was put to a more traditional use another day along 395. In the middle of nowhere, as most of 395 is, traffic stopped. It started backing up. Not moving at all. After maybe 15 or 20 minutes, a Highway Patrol car drove down the other side of the road and informed us that there had been a bad accident. We would not be moving again for at least an hour. If you study a map of eastern California, there are no alternate routes to 395. The few cars that turned around were in for a detour that would take many more hours. All we could do was turn off our engines and wait. People got out of their cars. I decided we should do something. I got out my Frisbee.

Someone pulled out a bag of chips. I had a few sodas in the car. Someone else had cookies. Soon we were having an impromptu picnic on the highway. It was a fun way to pass the time until things started moving again.

Rental Car Adventures

MY attempt to learn history at the Alamo could have gotten me killed. I toured the old mission which was the site of the famous battle in the Texas War for Independence. People had warned me to forget the Alamo, that it's not a good representation of what happened there. They were right, but I had to see it anyway. I have been to Gettysburg and Normandy and it is easy to picture the heroic events that took place on that hallowed ground. I got no such feeling at the Alamo. Too little of it has been saved and the roads and buildings encroaching make it hard to feel the past.

By the time I had toured the Alamo, the sun was fully up, and the Texas sun was hot. I decided to ditch my jacket in the rental car before strolling over to San Antonio's famous River Walk. I opened the trunk to my rented Mitsubishi and saw there was a lot of stuff in there. Stuff I didn't own. I figured the person who had previously rented the car had forgotten the items and I would report it when I returned the car. I tossed my jacket in the trunk and closed the lid. Then I noticed stuff in the passenger compartment as well. Stuff that was not mine and that I could not have failed to notice while driving the car from Austin earlier that morning. Something was weird.

I looked around and there was another red Mitsubishi parked about four cars away from this one. I went over and I looked inside. There were my map and sunglasses. I had put my jacket in the wrong car. But the key had worked. I now thought if I go back to retrieve my jacket, the actual owner of that car might return, see me "breaking" into their trunk, and this being Texas, might shoot first and ask questions later. I looked around very carefully and then quickly walked over, removed the jacket, and put it in my car.

Upon returning the car to—coincidentally—Alamo Rental Car, I told the counter clerk what happened with my key operating a different car. He said he wasn't surprised, and—I don't know if this is actually true—there are only about seven different Mitsubishi keys and that if they lose a key they just try a few to other cars until they find one that works. Seems a little sketchy to me. But if not for the random stuff in my car and some stranger's, I might have committed grand theft auto.

I always carefully look a rental car over for damages, a practice which has saved me more than once when the company has tried to charge me for a ding or scratch. I have been able to get the charges reversed by showing the rental forms on which I had noted the damage, including one time when there were several cigarette burns in the upholstery of a "nonsmoking" car.

One time before I drove a rental car off the lot, I noticed the car didn't have the little stickers in the upper corners of the license plate showing the month and year of expiration for the registration.

I went back to the rental car counter and told them. The clerk's attitude was a very casual, "So?"

I told him I wanted a car with stickers. He said, "Look around the lot. None of the cars have them. They get stolen all the time, so we stopped putting them on."

I said that it was illegal to not have the registration tabs properly displayed. He said that was not my problem. The car rental company would be the ones in trouble for that, not me. I told him I taught traffic school and I happened to know the law. I, as driver, would get the fix-it ticket if I was driving a car not in compliance with the law and even though I could likely have the ticket dismissed upon showing proof of registration, I didn't want the hassle of having to go through all of that.

I also didn't want to drive a car without the tabs because I had been on enough police ride-alongs to know how cops think. If they see two cars speeding, but one has a driver without a seatbelt, or a broken taillight, that car is more likely to get pulled over. They can get two or more tickets for one stop. I didn't want to be the wounded gazelle with the missing registration that would prompt a cop to pull me out of the herd.

The clerk seemed completely uninterested in my concerns. I finally flatly told him I would not rent the car without the stickers for the license plate. He grumbled something, then pulled out a set of keys, unlocked a drawer, and opened it. In it were hundreds of sets of stickers. He pulled out a set and handed them to me saying, "Here, knock yourself out."

I said, "Call me a skeptic, but I find it hard to believe that you were lucky enough to pick the right stickers for my car."

He said, "Huh?"

I pointed to the tiny numbers printed on the stickers perpendicular to where the month and year were more prominent. "These numbers match the registration to one of the cars on this lot. I'm doubtful that you got the right ones for the car I am renting."

He sighed. "And your point?"

I didn't have more time to argue and sighed. I took the stickers and illegally stuck them on the license plate and drove off. I knew it was extremely unlikely any police officer pulling me over was going to compare those numbers to the registration. I'd never seen a cop do that on all of my ride-alongs. I had registration on the car, if it didn't match that was definitely the fault of the company that owned the car, not the driver.

By the Time I Get to Phoenix

A friend in L.A. had an "uncle" in Phoenix. The guy was actually just a close friend of my friend's family, but he referred to him as his uncle. The uncle dealt in classic cars. Occasionally he'd find one of the rare cars in Southern California and would pay my friend to bring it to Phoenix for him. If I wasn't busy, I'd go along for the ride. That resulted in us getting to drive some interesting vehicles across the California desert.

The most fun we had was in a 1962 Jaguar XKE. It was the classic, low-cut Jag with the long nose. The specs said the car had a top speed of 150 mph and the speedometer went to 160. It is hard to get your hands on a car like that and not want to see which is accurate. I asked a friend who was a California Highway Patrol officer where it might be safe to open it up without getting a ticket or dying. He recommended Route 62, east of Joshua Tree National Park. Through traffic used I-10 from L.A. to Phoenix and anyone going to the Park wouldn't be going east of it on a road to the middle of nowhere. He said it was so lightly traveled that the CHP barely patrolled it any longer and if you did lose control of the car, going off the road would put you onto hard-packed dirt, so likely would not get you killed. Route 62 it was. Just had to be sure to fuel up before heading out there. Not a lot of towns or gas stations there.

One quirk about the XKE we were driving: the starter didn't work. To start the car, one person had to open the hood—not an easy task on this model Jaguar—clamp vise grips on the starter flywheel, and give it a good spin while the other person sat in the car and gave it some gas. It reminded me of the way it was once necessary to start airplanes with one person spinning the propeller while the other sat in the cockpit adjusting the choke and yelling "contact!" It was difficult to spin the flywheel sufficiently fast without your hand slamming into another part of the engine. This was especially painful after the engine had been running and the metal was hot.

After we had each injured our hands in the process, we opted not to shut off the engine again until we got to Phoenix. This meant violating the rule at the gas station about turning off the car while we refueled, and we even left the car running while we had lunch. We asked for a table by the window so we could keep an eye on the Jag, since it was unlocked and running with the keys in it. Even with its issues, the thing was worth $50,000 or thereabouts. We didn't want to lose it on the way to deliver it to its new owner.

We also didn't want to wreck it, but we did want to open her up and did, each taking a turn at the wheel on that deserted stretch of Route 62. We never got it above 140 mph, so both the specs and the speedometer lied. It was the only time I have come close to going that fast. It's very different going that fast in a car that was built for it. In the little cheap cars I had owned up to that point in my life, if I got above 80, the car was shimmying and the squirrels under the hood were screaming so badly it felt dangerous. The Jaguar handled so well that on a long, level straightaway with few landmarks to indicate speed, it was hard to tell how fast we were going without looking at the dashboard.

The other concern with the Jaguar was that driving to Arizona in the summer risked the danger of overheating. British cars are notorious for that, as well as engine fires. (There is the old joke: a cop pulls over a guy for speeding in his MG and says to the driver, "OK, pal, where's the fire?" and the driver says, "Under the hood!") We weren't sure how long we should leave the XKE running, especially while parked with no breeze to cool things down. If we broke down on that lonely stretch of road in these pre-cellphone days, it could be hours before another car happened by.

I was glad to get that boyish desire to speed out of my system in a quasi-safe way; I don't have to do it again.

On another car-delivery trip to Phoenix, we witnessed an incident that I thought about often during the 1992 L.A. Riots. I wondered if this technique had been employed would it have been possible to break up the unrest before it had a chance to catch hold.

My friend, his pseudo-uncle and aunt, and I were having dinner at a restaurant. When we went to leave, the owner of the restaurant said we probably didn't want to go outside just yet. Something was happening. He closed the horizontal window blinds so that if bricks started flying, glass wouldn't shower the restaurant. We peeked out the blinds. In the intersection that the restaurant faced, a confrontation was brewing. Two cars had apparently collided and two rival factions were gathering, about to face off over this incident. More people were gathering. I knew that insults and threats were being hurled in English and Spanish, though it was hard to hear much of what they were saying and what the issue was over the accident.

Would-be combatants were grabbing bricks and tire irons. I suspected a few people had guns or nearby access to them. Things were about to get very ugly when a Phoenix police car, lights and sirens blazing, came flying into the crowd, forcing the mob to part or get run over. The car skidded sideways to a halt and the lone cop jumped out of his black-and-white with a pump-action shotgun in hand. He leapt onto the hood of his car and discharged a round into the air over the roof of our restaurant. He got everyone's attention. There was a stunned silence until he bellowed, "If you were not driving this car or this car," he pointed to the crashed vehicles that blocked the intersection, "I want you out of this street by the time I count three!"

The leader of one of the two factions snapped back, "You can't shoot us all, asshole!"

Without missing a beat, the cop whirled around as he pumped another shell into the chamber, aimed the shotgun at the loudmouth's head and said, "No, but I can shoot you, asshole!"

There was only a half-second's pause as the crowd including the bigmouth digested that. The cop never even started counting, because the intersection was empty in under three seconds.

I suspect that cop's actions violated about 20 procedures of the police department, but damn was it effective. I contemplated that scene as I watched the L.A. Riots unfold on television. Maybe one brave, crazy cop with a shotgun and a complete disregard for the rulebook could have ended the Riots before they really got going.

Trouble on Tours

I get in trouble on tours. Maybe I should keep my big mouth shut, but sometimes when I am on tours, I just can't.

There was the tour I took of the U.S. Naval Academy with my brother and his sons. My nephew was a star wrestler in high school and was thinking of attending the famous school in Annapolis, which is known for their great wrestling team. With my interest in history, I wanted to tag along. As part of the tour, a midshipman took us into the Lawrence Ballroom. She explained that the room was named for Commodore James Lawrence, who as he was dying on the deck of his ship, uttered those famous words "Don't give up the ship."

She told us how Oliver Hazard Perry was so moved by Lawrence's words that he had a flag made bearing that motto and used it to inspire his men to win the Battle of Lake Erie. That flag and portraits of Lawrence and Perry hang prominently in the room. She went on to say that of course all of this happened during the American Civil War.

I couldn't help myself, and blurted out, "It did not!"

The whole tour group looked at me. Realizing that in my shock, I had been a bit rude I said, "I'm sorry, but it did not."

Even more surprised by my outburst than the rest of the tour was, the midshipman looked at me and said, "Sir?"

I said, "It didn't happen during the Civil War."

She said, "Sir?"

I said, "Ma'am, it happened during the War of 1812."

She said, "Sir, that's not what it says in our brochure."

"How could it have happened during the Civil War? Look at the death date on the portrait of Lawrence. He died in 1813."

She said, "Sir, that's not what it says in our brochure."

"And look at the death date for Perry; he was dead 40 years before the Civil War started."

She said, "Sir, that's not what it says in our brochure."

Getting frustrated, I asked, "Ma'am, what were we doing fighting the British on Lake Erie during the Civil War?"

She said, "Sir, that's not what it says in our brochure."

We went a couple of more rounds and the whole tour group was looking at me as though I was the idiot since she had the uniform and the brochure, so I turned to my brother whom I'm sure knows his history and I demanded, "Aren't you going to say anything?"

My ever-helpful brother replied, "Yes. Obviously you need to read their brochure."

Then there was the awkward moment at Wheatland, President James Buchanan's home in Lancaster, Pennsylvania. I asked if Senator William Rufus King of Alabama had ever visited the house. If I had relieved myself on the entry hall rug, the volunteer tour guide could not have been more offended.

When Buchanan was in the House of Representatives and King was in the Senate, they shared a room at a Washington, DC boardinghouse and were so clearly a couple that Andrew Jackson, who was president at the time, referred to them disparagingly as "Miss Nancy" and "Aunt Fancy." The newspapers of the era also made it clear that our country's only unmarried president wasn't exactly a "bachelor." Clearly the elderly tour guide at Wheatland was not going to acknowledge Buchanan's other life. A friend recently told me that when she visited Wheatland, she asked if it was true that Senator King's portrait hung in the house as long as Buchanan lived. My friend was met with the same apoplectic denial.

More trouble came at the Texas Capitol in Austin. I was asked to leave the tour. The guide in her prim uniform and pretty Texas-flag scarf said that Texas was the only state to have had six different countries' flags fly over it—the most of any state. I told her that wasn't correct, that California was the only state to have had six countries' flags fly over it. (If you're wondering: Spain, Mexico, England, Russia, the United States, and the California "Bear Flag" Republic.)

In Texas, they count the Confederacy as one of the six. I pointed out to the tour guide that the Confederacy was never a country. (That was one of their problems; if they had actually received foreign recognition or support, the Civil War might have ended differently.) However historically accurate it might be, telling a Southerner and a Texan that the Confederacy wasn't a country isn't necessarily a smart thing to do. She politely but firmly told me that I could now leave the tour and go read the Confederate Memorial and the memorial to General John Bell Hood on the grounds of the capitol to learn my history.

The lingering attitudes about the Civil War also got me in trouble while taking the tour of the campus at William & Mary. The student tour guide showed us the war memorials listing the W&M alumni who died in all of America's wars going back to before the founding of this nation. After he pointed out each plaque, including the fallen sons of the Confederacy, I said, "Many northerners also have attended the college. Where is this list of those who died fighting for the Union?" I was met with a cold stare and then a voice that suddenly became much more Southern: "Sir, if they did, we do not talk about them here!"

When I visit a place, I do my homework, wanting to know something of the area and its history. This can present a problem, especially when I end up knowing more than the tour guide. Someday I'll learn to behave. Probably not.

Then there was the visit to the Cabinet War Rooms underneath parliament in London. I was traveling with my then-roommate from Venice, California. To say history was not his strong suit would be generous.

Case in point:

He had never been east of Las Vegas and when I won a trip to New York City on the television game show *Jeopardy!*, he wanted to come along as my plus-one and since the prize package covered the airfare, hotel, and meals, he would cover all the incidentals: tours, taxis, subways, etc. After New York, we were going to take the train to Philadelphia to visit some of my college friends and then were going to drive across Pennsylvania to see some of the pretty countryside.

As we were planning the trip, we were discussing possible sights to see along the way. I suggested we stop in Gettysburg and he said, "That's cool. What's in Gettysburg?"

I was stunned and said, "You know, the battlefield?"

And he said, "Oh, they had a war there?

I said, "The largest battle ever fought in North America? You never heard of the Battle of Gettysburg?!?"

He said, "No. You just know all that history stuff."

And I said, yes, admittedly I knew a lot of arcane historic trivia, but *everyone* knew about the Battle of Gettysburg! It was one of the most important battles ever, anywhere!

I was still haranguing him about his incredible ignorance of history when his girlfriend walked in. He said, "I'll prove that you are the only one who knows this shit." He turned to her and said, "What is Gettysburg, Pennsylvania famous for?"

She said, "You're kidding, right? Everyone knows about Gettysburg!"

I said, "See???"

And she said proudly, sure she got the answer right, "That's where Benjamin Franklin signed the Gettysburg Address!"

I took a long breath to keep from screaming, and quietly said, "I beg of you, if you two get married, promise me you will never have children."

Spoiler alert! His knowledge of history was such that one time when he and I were watching the movie *Patton* I said I had seen it a few times and was going to bed. Besides I knew how it ended. Patton dies and the Allies win. He was upset because he had never seen the movie before and didn't know either of those things.

On a trip to Europe together, my roommate and I were taking the tour of the Cabinet War Rooms in London. These rooms deep under Westminster were occupied by Winston Churchill and his cabinet during World War II. They had offices there and met regularly to execute the war and carry out the duties of government. When the war ended, they were so glad to get away from that bunker, they left, and the rooms were pretty much forgotten about until 1984 and they were reopened to the public.

The wartime occupants had departed in a hurry, and no one wanted to go back down there, so the rooms were left pretty much the way they were in May of 1945. One of Churchill's cigars was still in its ashtray. There were half-smoked cigarettes and a half-eaten candy bar on other desks. Papers and pens were still strewn about. The place was frozen in time and gave a fascinating glimpse into the way the war was conducted, and into Churchill, and the way the world was then.

The tour guide was talking about how far underground the rooms were to be safe from the bombing and my friend turned to me and said, "Who was doing the bombing?"

The entire tour turned and gawked in shock at the cluelessness of the question. I was embarrassed to even have to answer and while I was debating if I should, he said proudly, sure he had the right answer, "Wait. Wait. I know this! It was World War II, so it was the Japanese, right?"

I summoned my best Spanish accent and said, "Lo siento, señor, pero no entiendo ingles."

The Hollywood Sign.

IV.

Brushes
with
Greatness

Hooray for Hollywood

I had only been in L.A. a couple of weeks and all of my pounding the pavement had yet to yield a job. I had applied for a job at a place on Hollywood Boulevard and was strolling back to my car, still marveling at the fact that I was really in Tinseltown. I could look up and see the famous sign on the hill. I could look down and see the stars in the sidewalk at my feet.

I came across a crowd of people and when I got closer, saw it was a ceremony to place a star in the sidewalk. The honoree was Henry Mancini. My parents loved him, in part because he was a fellow Pittsburgher, the son of a steelworker, as was my father. As I watched the speeches praising the composer of such great music as *Moon River* and the *Pink Panther* theme, I had a great idea. I had just been thinking about what to do about my parents' birthdays which were coming up soon since I barely had money for cards let alone presents. I dashed into a gift shop and bought a postcard that showed the stars of the Walk of Fame.

I positioned myself between the crowd and the waiting limo and as the crowd broke, I approached the man of honor and said, "Excuse me, Mr. Mancini, but my parents back in Pittsburgh are huge fans of yours and their birthdays are coming up. Could I trouble you to write 'Happy Birthdays Dorothy and Gil' on this card and sign it?"

He said he'd be happy to, and did. I thanked him and congratulated him. My parents had that post card standing on their bookcase for quite a while.

When I first moved to L.A. to break into the movie business, I knew no one and was starting from below square one. I knew less than nothing about Hollywood and had a lot to learn. My father warned me that he'd heard about some of the weird people out in California and that I should be careful. Through his work at the bank, he did know a couple of people with connections in show business and he would set up it up for me to meet them — separately — they didn't know each other.

The one client of my father's was just visiting her son, who worked in the movie business. He lived in the Hollywood Hills and she invited me to have dinner with them at the house one evening. The woman looked like she was auditioning to play Norma Desmond in a remake of *Sunset Boulevard*. Overdressed, overly made-up, and overly theatrical, she made quite a first impression. I was very naïve about gay people then, but it was clear from the moment I entered that the son and his *roommate* were a couple. Her son and his friend looked at my cute young self like lions assessing a raw piece of meat tossed into their cage.

One of them worked for one of the studios and said for years he had rescued films from the trash when he saw them thrown out. The couple had a few spare bedrooms that had been turned into vaults for storing hundreds of movies going back to the silents. One of the bedrooms was also set up as a screening room with a professional projection system and theater seats. He said in some cases he had only been able to find perhaps two of the six reels of a film, but he had a vast collection of movies I had never seen and wanted to. This was before there was a video rental store on every other corner and we could only hope to catch a classic was on the late-late-late show. They could tell I was thrilled to check out this much Hollywood history.

When it came time for dinner, there was a little jostling to see which of the guys sat next to me. We were not far into the meal when I felt a hand slide between my legs. Since both of my hands were on the table, this was a less than subtle come on from her son. I didn't want to cause a scene and possibly offend my father's client, so I spent the rest of the dinner discretely removing the extraneous hand from my lap. I made an excuse and left right after dinner. As I was leaving, the guys kept insisting I stay in touch and come over to watch some movies. As much as I did want to see some of those movies, I worried about what the second half of a double feature at their house might entail—especially if the mother was not there to chaperone.

I am not sure how well-connected those guys were in the movie business or if I missed a chance to meet some of the right people at the parties they said they had. I found it ironic that my father warned me about the creeps in Hollywood and he was getting me invitations to have dinner at their houses. I told him I had dinner there, but never told him the specifics.

I thought of that evening when, a year or so later, I met a young man while driving down Santa Monica Boulevard when I saw the familiar blue-and-yellow license plate from Pennsylvania. At the next stoplight I rolled down the window and asked the driver, "Where is Lansdowne?"

He replied, "I don't know. I'm not from around here."

"I was referring to your license plate frame. I'm from Pennsylvania and I never heard of Lansdowne." It was apparently the location of the dealership where he bought the car.

"Oh. Near Philly. Hey, do you want to get high?" He held up a joint.

I rarely got high, but I couldn't help noticing how cute he was. I said, "Sure!"

He motioned to the side street at the light. I nodded and when the light changed, he made a right turn, and I executed an illegal right turn from the left lane to follow him. He drove a couple blocks into a residential area where there was no traffic and few house windows facing the street. I parked and went to his car and when he motioned, got in the passenger seat.

He lit the joint and we introduced ourselves. I was still not out, even to myself, but I was struck by how handsome he was. Apparently I wasn't the only one who had noticed his attractiveness.

I asked if he had just moved to L.A. and he said he had planned to, but was leaving the next day to drive back to Philadelphia. He said a man approached him in Philadelphia and said he was a talent scout for actors and models and told this boyishly cute blond that he'd like to represent him. A few lunches and phone calls followed, and the guy convinced him to come to L.A. The boy was stuck in a job he hated in Philly and had always wanted to see California, so he said yes. After all, the guy even offered him a place to stay until he made some money.

The next part of the story wasn't surprising because I had heard enough variations of it, but usually with an attractive young lady at the center of it. When he got to the "agent's" house, the guy started plying the young man with alcohol and putting the moves on him. He fled the house, drove around for a while, and found a motel to spend the night. He was clearly still upset by the incident. He didn't say how far the assault got before he got away and I knew it was not my place to ask. He said he wanted to at least see Hollywood Boulevard and the Pacific Ocean before he left town. He had spent the day driving around to try to calm down and check things out before planning to drive back the next day.

He was shaken by what happened and I think he invited me to smoke with him to vent a bit, and as a fellow Pennsylvanian around his age (I was probably only three or four years older than he was), he thought he could trust me. We talked for about an hour. I was still so naïve about the gay world that I couldn't be sure if he was flirting or if I was excited or scared that he might be. After what he had been through, even if I'd known how to flirt with a hot guy, I wouldn't have done it. I was sorry he was leaving town the next day, but also understood that L.A. was already a bad memory.

We said goodbye and I never saw him again.

The other client of my father arranged for me to meet was much more normal and professional. She had helped produce a movie that was one of Denzel Washington's first starring roles, so she claimed a little credit for his start. She eventually did help me get my first job working on a TV show, *Tales from the Darkside*. She was nice enough to invite me to her quaint home in Benedict Canyon a few times. At one point she told me that a few doors down, right around the corner from her on Cielo Drive, was the house where Sharon Tate had been murdered. Having read *Helter Skelter* not long before this and I was still haunted by that macabre story, I had to go check out the house, not that there was much to see from the road. But it was still eerie to be so close to such a famous crime scene.

Tales from the Darkside

TALES from the Darkside was so low budget, they couldn't afford a sound stage and we shot inside an old mattress factory in the Boyle Heights section of Los Angeles. Mattresses were nailed to the exterior walls to soundproof the flimsy building. The show was produced by George Romero, who was famous for his low-budget horror movies, most notably the *Night of the Living Dead* series.

I thought it was ironic that I moved to L.A. to work in "the industry" and I ended up working for a company based in my hometown. Romero went to Carnegie Mellon University and shot his first movies in Pittsburgh. He had been to Hollywood a few times and hated it, so went back to Pittsburgh and ran things from there. He rarely came west. Some of the line producers he hired to run things for him were—uh…not the greatest guys to work for. But more of that later.

I was a Production Assistant, which on a set is the lowest of the low. We were the go-fers, clean-up people, runners, drivers, and on a low-budget shoot like this one, it meant we did anything anyone else wouldn't do. On a higher budget production, you wouldn't dare touch a light or camera, but here, if someone didn't show up for work, I became a gaffer, or assisted the best boy, or I was a stand-in for the star, or did whatever else they asked me to do. It was very educational. And sometimes quite fun. But long hours, a lot of work, and not great pay.

Each week the show would have a guest star; some were up and comers and some were a bit past their prime, but most were fun and interesting in their own way. Some of the other guest stars I had never heard of. IMDB didn't yet exist for me to be able to look people up and see why they looked familiar. Many I had heard of, I never got to interact with. After all, PAs do not speak to the star unless spoken to. In fact, as the most expendable person on the set, I was often out running around and never saw, let alone interacted with some of the stars. Besides knowing my place, I was much shyer then and didn't much speak to people unless spoken to.

There were many great moments from the season I worked for the show, but I'll start with Harry Anderson. Harry was the star of the new hit sitcom *Night Court*. He later did a bunch of guest roles on *Cheers* and starred in another successful sitcom, *Dave's World*, based on the writings of Dave Barry. Harry was a very down-to-earth, goofy and funny guy. He treated even the peon PAs with respect, which was not always the case with stars. He was generous. One night during the week he was on the show, he was performing at the Comedy and Magic Club in Hermosa Beach. He put the entire crew on the guest list and picked up the tab for our drinks. He was that kind of a guy. Between scenes, he was always telling jokes, doing magic tricks, and cracking us up.

One morning a bunch of us were sitting around waiting for the first scene to be ready to go. I was sitting in a corner reading the *Hollywood Reporter*, one of the industry newspapers. Harry was talking to a few of the other crew members. He was saying that he wasn't used to commuting to work as he had to for *Tales from the Darkside*. He said that he was probably the only person in the TV business who walked to work—he lived three blocks from where they shot *Night Court*. I went on reading, with the newspaper in front of my face, taking no part in the conversation. About 10 minutes later, I got up, casually tossed the paper on the table, and said, "Nothing of great interest in here. Just that Warner Brothers is moving all of their production facilities to Calabasas this season to save money."

I kept walking out of the room and then peeked back in as Harry lunged at the paper and tore into it looking for that news story. Then he looked again. And then a third time carefully combing the paper until it dawned on him. He looked up and saw me grinning. He loved the joke. (For those who don't know the L.A. area, Calabasas is about 30 miles west of Burbank where Harry lived, and it would be a horrendous drive out the 101 Freeway.) For the rest of the week Harry kept trying to get back at me with little jokes, but they always seemed to get interrupted by one of us being called away, so he never got even.

(Side note: years later, I taught traffic school in La Jolla to Reinhold Weege, the creator of *Night Court*. Of course we had to talk about what a great guy Harry was.)

Tippi Hendren was another very fun guest star. Although she has over 80 movies and TV shows listed on her IMDB page, most people remember Tippi from the two films she did for Alfred Hitchcock: *The Birds* and *Marnie*. Hitchcock had a thing for pretty blondes as his leading ladies, and according to most of them, including Tippi, he treated them horribly long before the "Me Too" movement called attention to such abuses. It must have been very hard for these women knowing that starring in a Hitchcock film would lead to stardom, but speaking out against one of the most powerful men in Hollywood would lead to career-killing oblivion. Tippi and I only talked about the fun side of her working with Hitch. It wasn't until much later that I learned about his horrendous actions and her being a victim of it.

A few months prior to my meeting Tippi, the Nuart Theater in West L.A. near where I lived in Venice, did a Hitchcock film festival. Every night for about 40 nights, they did a double feature—all of his films in chronological order except maybe a handful that were tied up in disputes over rights or something. Passes to the festival were inexpensive—it worked out to maybe $2 a night—and I only missed about five nights because of other obligations. Several nights they had a speaker who had worked on one of the movies, or a professor of film studies to provide insight and behind-the-scenes information, so I was very up on my Hitchcock when I was hanging out with Tippi.

I got to hang out with Tippi by accident. PAs do not hang out with the stars. There were several guests I barely saw, let alone spoke to because we were on such different levels with different jobs to do. It would be like a serf hanging out with the king. We shot a five-day week or if we were really far behind, sometimes had to work Saturdays to finish up. Early one week, Monday or Tuesday, I had to finish something up and when I emerged from the side area where I was working, everyone had gone to lunch. The place was empty. I was about to leave to get my own lunch, when I heard a door open and close. There was someone else left in the building. I looked, and it was Tippi coming out of her dressing room. Actually, to call it a dressing room is giving it far more than its due. It was a makeshift expanded closet.

It is a strict rule on TV and movie sets that the people on camera never go to lunch or eat in their costumes. They can't risk having them spill something on the dress they were wearing in the last shot and need to wear in the next shot. They are required to change before lunch. Tippi had gone into her room to change and had apparently taken a while, so people forgot about her and left. (A major faux pas to ignore your star.)

She asked me where everybody went, and I told her everyone was gone to lunch. She asked where to go to eat in this neighborhood. It was a rather scary-looking, rundown part of L.A. where businesses had bars on their windows and parking lots, including ours, were lined with tall fences topped by barbed wire. She said she didn't want to just go out wandering around looking for a place to eat, plus she wanted to be sure to be back for her afternoon call time. She was a professional and didn't want to be late.

I told her there were only a few places in the neighborhood that were very close and when I didn't bring my lunch (I often did, but hadn't that day), I usually went to a good taco place. She said that sounded fine and started to ask me where it was, then suggested we go together. How could I say no? Since I knew the way, she asked me to drive. We took my car and went for tacos.

We had a wonderful lunch, talking Hitchcock and other classic movies, sharing trivia and pointing out goofs in the movies—she told me about one I had never noticed in *Marnie* and now it jumps out at me every time I watch it. I had to remind myself that this was really happening—here I was having lunch with someone who had worked with some of the great Hollywood legends. She was friends with Sean Connery! She seemed to really enjoy talking to someone who knew their movies, too. We had to hurry back to the set so we weren't late.

The next day, she sought me out at lunchtime and asked if I wasn't busy, would I join her. Of course, I jumped at the chance. We were on our way out the door when one of the producers called me back. I excused myself from Tippi, hoping he wasn't going to make me go pick something up that was needed immediately and would make me miss my lunch date. Instead he asked me what I thought I was doing. He yelled at me saying that PAs do *not* have lunch with stars and I'd better know my place, etc. What the hell did I think I was doing? I told him that Miss Hendren had asked me to have lunch with her and I thought it would be rude to say no. I knew we were supposed to keep our stars happy. Then he yelled at me for keeping Miss Hendren waiting, and if she asked me then Go! GO! Why are you standing around? He was very much like that as I would discover time and time again.

Tippi and I had really fun lunches the rest of the week. She wanted me to meet her daughter. (Her daughter is actress Melanie Griffith, whose career was just starting to take off, but pre-*Working Girl*, the movie that would make her a household name.) And Tippi suggested I come up to her ranch north of L.A. at some point. The "ranch" was a game reserve where she worked taking care of tigers and lions that had been used in movies and were in danger of being destroyed. These days it would be so easy to stay in touch with texting, email, and Facebook, but back then we just had each other's phone numbers. I got busy (working for the show and working another job on weekends, trying to make ends meet as I established myself in L.A.) and it was a few weeks before I had time to possibly visit. And by then it just seemed like it would be weird to call her up and say, "Hey, remember me, I want to come stay at your ranch!" I was much shyer back then. Now I would call. And of course now, it would be so easy to send an email. But thus ended my fun week with Tippi.

One other example of the producer's mercurial behavior was when we had an ex-NBA player as our big-name guest star for the week. I will not mention the NBA star because of part of this story. He was a super-nice guy, but man could he not act.

Some weeks, I had to play chauffeur to the guest star. Sometimes that meant picking them up in my crappy little car and sometimes that meant picking up a limo and then picking up the star. This producer claimed credit for scoring the major coup of landing the basketball player to be on the show. He warned us that the NBA guy was there as a personal favor to him—although I doubt that was true, because it later became clear that they didn't know each other—I was there when they met. He told us we should not bother the athlete. No photos, no autographs. Everyone on the crew was totally professional so such a warning was unnecessary and really indicated that he didn't know much about us or what he was doing.

The producer was so eager to meet the NBA guy that he wanted me to pick him up first in the limo, so he could ride to the sound stage with the guy and have some alone time. That already didn't make me happy since it meant I'd have to get up half an hour earlier to go get him. But I did as I was told. Then I went to pick up our star in a high-rise tower in Westwood. As I turned out of the driveway, I made a left onto Wilshire Blvd. The glass panel between the driver's seat and the rear compartment opened up and the producer began yelling at me. Didn't I know where the hell I was going? The sound stage was toward downtown! Why the hell was I headed west? Was I an idiot? I calmly explained that since the 405 was less than a mile west, it would be faster to jump on the 405 and take it south to the 10 rather than wind surface streets down to the 10.

The basketball guy spoke up and said that it would definitely be faster to take the 405. That was the route he always took downtown. The producer, acting as though he had never heard my explanation, said, "He <using the star's first name as though they were old friends although I had just seen them meet less than five minutes prior> has a great idea—why don't you take the 405 to the 10?"

I couldn't say a word and even if I wanted to, because he slammed the glass shut. I watched in the mirror as the basketball star gave the producer the side-eye and shook his head. Clearly they were not going to be friends.

When we got to the mattress factory, I was shocked by what I saw in the producer's office. Stacked floor to ceiling along one wall were basketballs. At least 50 of them. There may have been 100. And the producer wanted the star to sign them all! After telling us not to ask for anything, he brought in dozens of balls for autographs. Perhaps he had pre-arranged this with the star, but I very much doubt it. I don't know if they ever got signed or not.

The basketball great sought me out to thank me for the ride and said he was sorry about the way I had been treated. He said he told the producer that was no way to treat anyone, ever. Then he said he had a favor to ask. He said he appreciated the limo, but given his height, he'd really appreciate it if we could get a stretch limo for the following day. I said I didn't know, but I would check.

I went to the producer who I knew would have to authorize such an expense and arrange for a stretch. Of course he yelled at me again, saying I didn't have the authority to make such decisions, who did I think I was, etc. I explained that I had not made any decision, that I told the star I would check, and that is what I was doing. Then he yelled that of course we'd get the star a stretch limo, what kind of idiot was I? The next day I didn't have to repeat the drive because they did get a bigger car for our guest and you need a different class license to drive a stretch. I was happy I didn't have such a license for many reasons.

The reason for omitting the star's name is this: although he was a very nice guy, courteous to me and everyone else on the set, he couldn't act. Not even a little bit. All week long it was painful to listen to him try to deliver his lines which at best were monotone and at worst were flubbed over and over again. It had been a long week as they had to do take after take after take.

After watching professionals including Tippi Hendren and Keenan Wynn usually nail their parts on the first take, it was especially painful to hear the sad delivery. I was glad I was off set more than I was on so I didn't have to listen to the bad acting. But I was there Friday night when the star had to deliver his big speech. A long speech, maybe eight or ten lines of complicated verbiage. And he simply couldn't get it. They tried cue cards, coaching, everything they could think of. The crew was eager to go home. It was getting late, we were tired and frustrated. And as he would try again, those of us on the back side of the flimsy fake walls could hear him start and we'd begin mouthing the words along with him, hoping the movement of our lips would somehow carry to his mouth and he could finish the speech. We paced behind the wall as we mouthed the words over and over again only to hear the director yell cut after another bad take.

After a particularly bad take, the director yelled, "Cut! That's a wrap!" The crew looked at each other in shock. Clearly that was not a useable take. But the people around the camera were already running out of the room and headed for the exits. I had to get some information from the director, I forget what, but I couldn't leave until I had done so. When I approached him, he looked distraught. After asking my necessary question, I said, "Why did you wrap? I didn't hear one useable take."

I thought he was going to cry. He said, "I just gave up. We're all tired, and it was never going to get any better. We'll try to fix it in post. Maybe there is a way to edit together one useable speech from all those takes. Or maybe we can just record him reading the script, but I just couldn't take it anymore. The crew couldn't take it anymore." He hung his head in desperation.

These were mainly young directors, just starting out, and they really wanted to do a great job with the meager resources so they could show this as a sample of their work. In most of their cases, it was one of their first times helming a project. I knew this director was concerned that this poor performance would reflect badly on him. I had seen that NBA guy in some movies and he wasn't good, but he wasn't terrible, so maybe it was a bit this director's fault that he couldn't coax an adequate performance out of him.

I often had to take canisters of film to have the color corrected, sound or special effects inserted, pick up more film, etc. I was new to L.A. and very dependent on my Thomas Guide. Everyone in L.A. had one. A thick book of street maps with an index by which everyone navigated in that primitive pre-GPS world.

I was still getting used to driving in the area and I remember having to take a script to actor Dick Miller at his home way up in the Hollywood Hills. The roads kept getting steeper and narrower, reminding me of some of the mountain slopes above the South Side of Pittsburgh, and I found myself wondering how the hell they got a snowplow up Dick Miller's street in the winter. Then I remembered they probably don't get all that much snow in that part of Southern California. Dick Miller is one of those actors like George Petrie, who also did a guest shot on *Tales from the Darkside*, who is recognizable from their dozens of great character roles they did although many people may have never known their names.

Some of my trips outside the make-shift sound stage were fun. If we needed a car for a scene, I was usually the one dispatched to get it. One day that meant driving what was at the time the most expensive, flashiest Mercedes convertible out there. I had so many people checking me and the car out as I flew down the Santa Monica Freeway, I'm sure a lot of them wondered who this kid was who could afford a car like this. They probably thought I was the spoiled son of a Hollywood mogul.

Being on the road a lot as part of the job had me miss seeing Farley Granger and Peggy Cass at all. I saw, but never interacted with stars Vic Tayback, (famous for *Alice*); Danny Aiello (before he did the movie that made him famous, *Do the Right Thing*); Alice Ghostley (who did dozens of movies including *To Kill a Mockingbird* and *The Graduate* and many TV shows, but whom I remembered best as Esmeralda on *Bewitched*); Dick Shawn (best known for *The Producers*); Vince Edwards, (*Ben Casey*); and Fritz Weaver, (who also did a million acting gigs and often played characters who were scary and although I never talked to him, he did seem intimidating).

(Side note about Vince Edwards. Later I took a screenwriting class at Santa Monica College and the guy teaching the class had been a writer on the TV show *Ben Casey*. I told the teacher that I had worked on a show with a friend of his. He asked who. I said Vince Edwards. He said, "What makes you think he was a friend of mine?" I answered because they had worked together on *Ben Casey*. His response still sticks with me: "We were not friends. In a business populated by nothing but egos and assholes, Vince Edwards was in a class by himself.")

There were a couple of other stars with whom I did at least get to speak. Justine Bateman was at the height of her cutest *Family Ties* popularity. She was very nice to everyone. One of the crewmembers was so smitten with her, he violated the rule about the crew not fraternizing with the talent. He asked her out. They dated for over a year.

The other Hollywood legend who was fun to work with was Keenan Wynn. As the son of actor Ed Wynn, Keenan was born to the business. One day while some of the crew were taking a good bit of time to set up the special effects for the next scene, Keenan sort of held court telling stories of his decades of working in the business. He had been in so many movies and TV shows, he might have been the Kevin Bacon of his day, crossing paths with so many stars. He said that with all of those credits the two roles that people most wanted to talk about, would stop him in the grocery store to talk about, were Colonel Bat Guano in the classic film *Dr. Strangelove,* and as the writer who kills Rod Serling in an episode of *The Twilight Zone.* With all his roles, he was very humble, referring to himself not as a movie star, but as a craftsman whose job it was to support the lead actors.

(Side note: *Dr. Strangelove* is one of my all-time favorite movies, so I was thrilled to meet the guy who delivered one of my favorite lines in any film ever: "But if you don't get the president of the United States on that phone, you're going to have to answer to the Coca-Cola company.")

The season ended and now I had a choice to make. What to do? By the last few weeks of the show, most of the crew was scrambling to try to line up their next gig. It is a weird business. While we were shooting, everyone was complaining about the long hours and looking forward to a day off. Now that lots of days off were coming, everyone was panicking. I had already noticed this about the business including with my landlady at the time who worked on movies. She complained about the 12- 16- 18-hour days, wanting the movie to end so she could just rest. Then the minute the movie wrapped she started worrying about when the next gig would come! How would she pay her rent? Feed her kids? In that business there is either too much work or not enough work. There is rarely such a thing as just the right amount. More on my landlady in a story for another time.

I had no money saved up and I needed a job right away. I couldn't afford to wait around in hopes of getting another gig. Everyone was networking with everyone else, trying to see who was doing what and who might bring them along. I got a few inquiries about what I was doing next and if I might be interested in a possible something-or-other. But they were all just possibilities, nothing definite that would start in the next week or two, which was what I needed.

There was another thing about staying in the business. I had moved to Los Angeles to be a screenwriter. I naively thought I would show up with some scripts under my arm, studios would buy them, and I'd be set. I had no idea how hard it was to get an agent or actor or producer to read a script by an unknown, let alone get them to make it. I was working long, hard hours on the set. Many days I had to be on the set at 6 a.m.. Sometimes I wouldn't get off until 9 or 10 p.m. Then I had a 45-minute drive home. Pack lunch for the morning, get up, shower and do it all again. If I took another similar gig, after just one season of experience, I was unlikely to move up much in the credits. I would still be making very little money—and I would still have no time to write or to try to sell my writing. As it was, I was working another job on weekends which left no time for laundry and grocery shopping or catching up on sleep or writing.

I got another job. This was another crossroads where I wonder what would have happened if I had stayed more deeply involved in the business. Many people who started with me, or who were just a rung or two above me on the ladder, went on to successful careers. Some as sound or prop or camera crew. But none as writers or directors or actors. Although one of the Pas who started with me rose through the business and went on to produce *Band of Brothers* and *The Pacific*. So who knows?

Remembering "The Sheik." Really?

A few years after I moved to L.A., a friend-of-a-friend from Penn State invited me to join her at an odd event. Every year, on the anniversary of Rudolph Valentino's death, the Hollywood Forever Cemetery, his resting place, has a memorial service for him. For years the commemoration was a serious affair with actors and crew who had worked with him speaking about their time on set with the man who would go down in history as *The Sheik* after his most famous role.

But at this time, 60 years after his death in 1926, at age 31, at the height of his looks and fame, finding people to speak at his memorial who actually had anything to do with Valentino was getting harder and harder. The guest speaker the year we went to his memorial was a guy—I am not making this up—whose great-uncle played the organ in a movie theater that once showed a Valentino film.

For years the "Lady in Black," her face and identity hidden by a veil, would come and periodically place flowers at his Valentino's crypt, and on the day of the memorial would come and weep loudly and copiously over her lost love. The original Lady in Black claimed to be one of the Latin Lover's last lovers. The original Lady in Black died in 1984 and the woman who showed up to weep over Valentino's grave the year I went was allegedly her grandniece, according to one attendee at the memorial. But with her period costume and veil, it was hard to know. I guess the mystery was part of the aura of the occasion.

The Sheik had a couple of wives and a string of alleged mistresses, but more recent rumors have circulated suggesting that Valentino had affairs with at least as many men as women, including possibly his rival as king of the silent screen's Latin Lovers, Ramon Novarro.

Far from legitimate grieving for a fallen screen idol, the annual memorial had descended into farce. The few people who were crying real tears—how could they be grieving so deeply for a stranger who was dead before they were born?—were far outnumbered by those of us who had come to observe this odd bit of performance art. The tears we were shedding were from giggling, not bereavement. The whole thing, but especially its self-conscious attempts at solemnity, seemed ridiculous.

We did feel a odd about laughing so hard in a chapel during a memorial, and there is the old expression about laughing in a church: it seems so inappropriate that the harder we tried to stop, the more we found ourselves snickering. We decided to step outside to try to control ourselves. We sat down on a bench to try to get laughed-out before we went back inside.

An older woman came up to us and said, "It's lovely isn't it?" We weren't quite sure what she meant, and our puzzled looks must have given away our confusion. She said, "Tyrone Power's grave. You're sitting on it."

We jumped up. And there was his Shakespearean epitaph. "Good night sweet prince and flights of angels sing thee to thy rest."

She said, "It's okay. He clearly meant it to be used as a bench. I went to his funeral."

I asked, "Oh? Did you know him?"

"Oh, no. I just go to celebrity funerals. I've been doing it for years."

According to his gravestone, Power had died in 1958, so apparently she had.

She then went on to give us a list and a partial review of some of the famous funerals she had attended. "When Chico Marx died in 1961, I went to his funeral at Forest Lawn, Glendale. It was disgraceful. His brothers were laughing and clowning the whole time. So disrespectful."

I was thinking, who the hell are you to tell his brothers how to grieve? The Marx Brothers made a good living out of zany comedy. I never knew them, but I suspected that might have been the sendoff Chico would have wanted Groucho and Harpo and Zeppo and Gummo to give him.

She got teary-eyed mentioning a few of the more moving ceremonies she had attended. She was still angry about Bing Crosby's funeral almost a decade earlier. She said, "They held it at a ridiculously early hour at an 'undisclosed location' to try to keep it private. But I found out and I went anyway. They only wanted family and his closest friends, but I thought that was wrong. I thought his fans should be there."

I was incredulous. "Wait? You crashed Bing Crosby's funeral???"

"Yes. It wasn't right of them to try to keep people out."

I was flabbergasted. Hers was an odd hobby to say the least, but now it clearly had crossed the line into bat-shit crazy.

My friend and I excused ourselves to go back inside. I don't think she knew we had been giggling, but she admonished us anyway, "I hope you're here to grieve. It is so offensive that people laugh at this solemn ceremony. I know I will end up crying again. I come every year."

She made us feel creepy about even being there. We were more subdued when we went back inside, and we never attended the memorial again.

I Don't Know WTF Micky Dolenz Is Talking About

WHEN I was living in Venice and teaching traffic school, I was in rather good shape, and apparently fairly attractive. I was once just walking down the beach and had a photographer come up to me and ask if I would like to do some modeling. I rarely wore a shirt when I lived in Venice. It was a beach community, so no one thought it odd if you went to the bank or post office topless, and I kind of liked the looks I got from both guys and girls.

Back in my modeling days.

I was in a few low-budget TV commercials, including one for Catholic cable television in which I played a Marine far from home and the only thing that kept me going was being able to watch Catholic cable TV. I wish I had a video of this, with me in the tight green T-shirt and camo pants watching TV.

I was in a couple of low-budget movies that never got finished. For a little while I went on some auditions, but I never got any gigs that I went into cold. I decided I'd had enough rejection through the mail for my writing that I didn't need it in person for acting or modeling. But if someone was willing to pluck me off the beach or out of a traffic school class and pay me, I wouldn't say no.

I had a traffic school student approach me and say that he was making a video for a new center to help homeless people. He would like me to play one of the counselors whose job it would be to help get people whatever assistance they needed in terms of addiction counseling, housing, nutrition, and employment. The video gig didn't pay very well, but it seemed like a good cause. And it might be good for the acting reel I was starting to assemble.

The person who would be walking through the center asking each of the counselors about their jobs would be Micky Dolenz. Having grown up with *The Monkees*, how could I turn down a chance to meet him?

When I got to the set, the producer-director who had hired me, welcomed us all and he said Micky would be there any minute. He said Micky was not getting paid anything for doing this shoot and thus he wanted to show Micky appreciation and respect, so please, please do not bring up *The Monkees*. That is all anyone wants to talk to him about, so please, cut him some slack and keep it professional.

But how can you meet a Monkee and not be thinking about that constantly? Every time Micky would leave the room, someone would start quietly singing, "Hey, Hey, we're the…" and everyone else would start quietly singing along until Micky came back in and we'd all shut up as though we were totally innocent. I think he suspected.

The premise of the video was that Micky would tour the facility and talk about what would happen in each area. He would stop and talk with the actors who were portraying the people working there.

I was playing the job counselor and Micky came into "my office," sat on the edge of my desk and asked a question. It was not the question in my script, but close enough so I adapted my line to fit the question. I thought, okay, Micky wants to improv. He is the professional here, if he wants to go off the script, he can.

He asked me another question that was even further afield and not really related to what I was supposed to be doing or saying. But I managed to bluff an acceptable answer. But his next question required an answer I couldn't fake. "And exactly how much will this cost per client? Give me a dollar figure."

Knowing I couldn't make up a number when he clearly wanted the right one, I knew there was only one thing to do. I had been on enough sets to know that by late in the day after everyone has been working too long, they could use a laugh. I looked Mr. Dolenz in the eye and said, "I have to tell you, Micky, I have no fucking clue."

He slipped off the end of my desk, he was laughing so hard. When he could speak again, he said, "What was that?"

And I said, "I'm sorry, Micky, I don't know what page you're on, but those are not my questions." I reached into my desk drawer and pulled out my sides and handed the four sheets of paper to him.

He looked at them and said, "Oh! You're right. I was doing the wrong section. Those questions are for the next guy. I'm sorry!" He turned to the director, apologized again and asked if we could take it again. We did and nailed it one take. Micky is a pro. And I knew I had my few lines down.

Once we wrapped that scene, the director thanked me and said I could go home. He also said he almost lost it when I ad-libbed my little smart-ass line. He wasn't sure what I was doing, and he didn't laugh until after it became apparent why I did it. Then he laughed and appreciated the joke as a way to break the tension—and he loved that Micky loved it.

Somewhere I have a VHS tape of the shoot, but unfortunately it doesn't have the outtakes.

A few years later, Micky's daughter Ami, who is an actress, was in one of my traffic school classes. I told her to ask her father about that little moment we shared, but don't know if she ever did.

Shirley You Can't Be Serious

ONE day in 2002, I had a man approach me after a traffic school class in San Diego and ask me if he could hire me to MC an event for his charity. It was a charity to support youth and they were having a high-dollar, black-tie fundraiser at the Friars Club in Beverly Hills. The gig wouldn't pay all that well, but I jumped at the chance to go to the famous institution.

The Friars Club has since gone out of business and their building was razed, so I am even more grateful that I had a chance to experience the institution. I grew up watching the Dean Martin celebrity comedy roasts from the Friars Club. All of the Hollywood legends had played that room: Bob Hope, Jack Benny, George Burns, Judy Garland, Sammy

Davis Jr, the Marx Brothers, John Wayne, Jimmy Stewart, Redd Foxx, Foster Brooks, Phyllis Diller, Johnny Carson and so many more. The club was founded by Milton Berle. I can still remember Red Buttons' great "he never got a dinner" routines and Rich Little's impressions they did on the stage.

When I pulled into the parking lot at the Friars Club, I was already embarrassed. They only had valet parking and I had to turn my old Toyota over to the guy who was used to parking BMWs, Rolls, and Porsches. He looked at my car like I had just asked him to pick up my dog's poop.

The Friars Club was already past its prime as so many of its lustrous members had already passed on and it wasn't attracting a younger crop of famous members. But I was surprised what bad shape it was in. The wallpaper was peeling in places. My chair had cigarette holes burned in it and parts of the upholstery were threadbare. The tablecloth had rips in it that had been poorly repaired. The cloth napkins had seen better days and the silverware and plates looked old and worn out. That was a bit disappointing. Having admired the Friars Club from afar, and having it be less Versailles and more dying family restaurant was sad.

I had written my talking points to have (I hoped) funny opening remarks and then share information about the youth program. When I got there, I took note of some of the notables who were in attendance, including Jonathan Winters, Frankie Avalon, the designer of the Batmobile (George Barris), Mr. Blackwell, and others. I quickly added some clever remarks about them to be able to recognize their presence, but also, I hoped, get a laugh. The biggest name there, whom I would be excited to meet, was Shirley Jones, (Mrs. Partridge). She was there with her husband, comedian Marty Ingels.

The show would be opened by a woman who was the host of *Inside Hollywood*, or *Extra* or one of those types of shows. I never watched TV, let alone celebrity gossip shows, so I hadn't heard of her, but apparently this very pretty blonde was a big name and a big deal. Strangely my program from the event lists the other guests, but doesn't have her name or mine. The plan was that because she was a busy star, she had agreed to open the show but then had to dash off to another event or work or something and I would MC the show.

I figured she would just say her part, then introduce me and dash off and then I would do my cute little opening remarks. But I was about to learn something amazing about the way all of those Hollywood connections work. I used to watch *The Tonight Show* or those celebrity roasts or any awards show and wonder how everyone in the entertainment business knows each other and is such close friends. They don't. They aren't.

She welcomed me up on stage and gave me a kiss on the cheek and started to joke with me in a way that indicated our close friendship. She teased me in an intimate way that I am sure left everyone in the room thinking we had just been to a party together the night before, that I was probably at a barbecue by her pool last week, and that she and I had lunch together often. We may even have dated once or twice. Such was our warm familiarity.

Having no choice but to answer in kind, I teased back. We bantered back and forth for a few minutes before she took her leave. I realized all of those close Hollywood friendships were as real as the one she and I had. The depth of our deep relationship was exchanging about six words before she took the stage.

No one in that room could possibly have heard of me, but to have the stamp of approval of this well-known TV hostess I'm sure made them think I was someone, so as much as she left me befuddled, she had done me a huge favor by raising me to her equal in their eyes.

She had me so occupied that it wasn't until she was gone and I was alone on stage that I turned to fully face the audience and realized what a predicament I was in. Her fun and funny routine had completely pre-empted the opening I had prepared. While I stood there smiling, I tried to sort out in my mind if there was any way to segue from where she had left me to the comments I wanted to open with. There was none.

And then the other half of my dilemma struck me. While she was on stage and occupying all of my attention, I had not noticed the other problem: I couldn't see or hear the audience.

The lights were so bright in my eyes, I could see nothing. Not a person or table or wall.

Had they really stopped applauding already for the woman leaving the stage? That didn't seem likely. But if they weren't applauding, I was now standing there in silence. Deer-in-the-headlights silence.

(Side note. People wonder why comedians always pick on the people in the front row. Having been on stage a few times in clubs, I can tell you: it's likely they are the only people they can see. You have bright lights in your eyes and some of that light spills over into the front row so you can see those faces, but beyond that is usually back-of-a-cave blackness.)

I was now on stage alone in the lights and I had to say something. I might be shutting down her applause, but decided awkward silence was even worse at a show like this. I took a breath and said something. I don't remember what and I remember thinking it probably wasn't very good.

And now my next problem hit me. There were speakers across the foot of the stage and all I could hear was my own voice. The room was seemingly silent. None of the house noise was making it up to me. Now I not only couldn't see if they were laughing or applauding, I couldn't hear if they were. Maybe there was just silence. Did I really suck that bad?

I did a rather sloppy transition from what I had just said to one of what (I thought) was one of the best jokes in my bit. Silence. It hit me that if I was dying, perhaps silence was appropriate for my funeral. But I still couldn't believe there was no reaction at all. I tried another line. Should've gotten a big laugh. All I could hear was my own voice coming out of those damn speakers in front of me.

I still can vividly remember the faucet of sweat that started running down my spine. I could feel the top of my tux pants getting wet. I now had this fear that my pants would get so wet that it would look like I had peed myself. And the way I was feeling, I was also wondering if there was a possibility I would. As though I needed one more thing to fear. It wasn't flop sweat; it was a flop deluge. I had never sweated like that on stage ever. The hot lights weren't helping.

Every time I said something, I sweated the few seconds of silence, not sure if I was facing dead air, or if when I started talking I would be cutting off my own laughter and applause.

I had my cute little remarks about the TV stars present, but hadn't taken note of where they were sitting and now it would seem weird to just address the room at large. I assumed I would be able to look at them while talking about them. For all I know, they may have left the room.

Luckily as I was mounting the stage, just before I was blinded by the light, (cue Manfred Mann), I caught sight of Shirley Jones sitting in the front row at the far side of the stage. Once on stage I could no longer see her but just had to hope that somewhere in the whiteness she was still there. I faced her general direction, thanked her for coming and told her that I had once seen her perform at South Park at the Allegheny County Fair when I was child and that my parents, as fellow Pittsburghers, always went to see her when she played Heinz Hall. I then made some cute little quip about *The Partridge Family*, still unsure if I was really talking to her or just the white out.

I will always be grateful to Shirley's husband, Marty Ingels, who jumped on stage to banter with me about what I had just said. I had been facing the right direction! He came out of the whiteness where I thought they were! He was laughing and clearly had been enjoying what I was saying. We teased back and forth a bit before he resumed his seat. The interaction and the look on his face that he was having a good time made me relax a lot. I said a few more of my clever (I hoped!) remarks, introduced the next act, and then left the stage—without pretending to be best friends with the musicians taking the stage.

Years later, when I was telling this story, a friend who is very well-connected in Hollywood and knew Marty, said Marty was such a nice guy, and, as a fellow comedian may have sensed my distress and come to my rescue. If that is true, I am even more grateful to the now-late Mr. Ingels.

Somehow, I survived my stage time at the Friars Club, but I am sure I sweated out about 20 pounds of fear. I was so traumatized the whole time I was there, so I do not remember who the other celebrities present were or any of the jokes I used that evening, which according to the people I spoke to after, did get laughs.

I knew my parents, who really were big fans of Shirley would never forgive me if I didn't get a photo with her. I rushed to catch up with her and Marty as they were leaving, and he was nice enough to take a photo of Shirley and me outside the club. My parents had that picture enlarged and framed and kept it on a bookshelf in their TV room for the rest of their lives.

After the show, the guy who had hired me asked me how I knew the woman who had brought me on stage. He assumed, as I am sure had most people in the audience except those in show business, that she and I were old friends. I told him I had never met her until a minute before I set foot on stage, but I had no choice to play along with her script. He was surprised I was making it up on the spot and thought she and I played so well together that we obviously knew each other and had planned that interaction. He thought we were hilarious together.

(Side note about the folks in the audience. Several were Romanovs. The guy who had hired me ran the youth charity with his wife who was a Russian countess or duchess or some high-ranking member of the Russian Royal family. She explained the connection to me: apparently her great-aunt was one of several people with a claim to the Russian throne if the royal family is ever restored. The woman I was dealing with might have been twentieth or something in line to the throne, not that it really mattered. I don't think any of them will be ruling Russia again anytime soon, but several of them float around in Beverly Hills high society.)

Not Knowing Paul Sorvino

A lot of people on the periphery of Hollywood claim to be further along in their careers and better-connected than they actually are. I saw a great example of that one afternoon at the Starbucks in West Hollywood. I was writing a screenplay on my laptop when the guy at the next table, recognizing the formatting unique to screenplays, asked me what my script was about. I told him. He said he was also a screenwriter. He said one of his scripts was going to star Paul Sorvino. He had been meeting Paul for months, honing the script; a studio was interested, and they hoped to be shooting by October. It all sounded very exciting and promising. I couldn't tell if he was telling me all of this to try to one-up me, (although I hadn't told him where my project was in terms of getting it made), or if he was using his bigger success in the business as a way of flirting with me. While he is telling me about his close relationship and the big plans he is making with Paul Sorvino, who walks into the Starbucks but Paul Sorvino.

If we had scripted it and rehearsed it, this scene could not have played out any better. I was facing the door and saw Paul come in carrying a script and some other papers under his arm. I said to the guy, "Well, isn't this a coincidence?"

He asked, "What's that?"

I said, "Paul Sorvino just walked in."

The guy got a shocked look on his face, then his head did a quick pivot to confirm that it was true and quickly turned back to me. "Oh," he said.

I asked if he wasn't going to go say hi to Paul. He said, no, he hated to bother him.

I said, "He looks bored in line. I'm sure he'd be happy to see you." The lines at that Starbucks are always at least 10 people long. I would want someone I knew to keep me company in line if that were an option. As Sorvino took his place in the queue, the guy kept looking away from the line. It became apparent he was afraid that if Paul looked our way and didn't acknowledge his work colleague that I would know for sure what I had suspected—that this guy had never met Sorvino and certainly wasn't working on a movie with him.

While watching the guy sweat about being caught in his little lie, I kept an eye on Sorvino so I could wave at him and call attention to his alleged co-worker. I pressed the guy, "I'd love to meet Paul. Maybe you could introduce me?" He again said he hated to bother the star. I said Paul looked bored and I promised to be polite and not say trite things about *Goodfellas*. He again made excuses as to why we shouldn't bother Paul.

After Paul got his order, he did glance our way. I didn't wave, but I did nod hello. I'm sure he saw us, and if he really knew this guy, he'd have recognized him, and if he wasn't going to come say hello he would have at least kept his eyes on us longer as you would do when you see someone you know in public. Paul left and the guy seemed a little relieved. Now that he was clearly caught in his bullshit, I excused myself to go back to work on my script.

Afterward, I thought about what a perfect person Sorvino was for this guy's gambit. If he had said he was working with one of the biggest stars in Hollywood—DiCaprio, Streep, Hanks, Pitt—I would have instantly been skeptical. But Sorvino was a big enough name to be instantly recognizable yet at the same time, believable. I wonder if the guy ever bragged about his Sorvino movie deal again. It's too easy to get caught in Hollywood.

The Gimp is Hard to Recognize When in Costume

WHEN the movie first came out, I saw *Pulp Fiction* with some friends in L.A. Since they were actors, they always stayed for the credits. And they saw the name of an actor friend of theirs in the credits. But somehow, they had missed him in the movie, so they wanted to stay and watch it again, which we did. The reason they didn't recognize him—he was the gimp! The guy in the leather bondage outfit who was kept in a trunk by the bad guys in the movie.

The Son of the Angel of Death

THIS story is no about greatness, but rather infamy. When I was working a motel in Venice, California I had encounters with a few interesting people, but none more disturbing than my encounter with the son of the Angel of Death.

In 1985, it hit the news that Josef Mengele, the doctor infamous for his inhuman treatment of prisoners at Auschwitz, had died a few years earlier. He had drowned off the coast of Brazil and had been buried under a false name.

I had just been watching the news about this when a man came to check into the motel. He filled out the registration form and I barely glanced at the name. I checked in so many people. He had a German accent so it didn't surprise me when I asked for ID, as we required of all guests, and he produced a German passport. Then his name hit me: Rolf Mengele.

Mengele is not a common name and having just seen it on the news, I couldn't help but wonder if there was a connection. But I didn't say anything. What could I say? Hey, are you any relation to one of the most evil people of all time?

That evening I was watching *Nightline*. Ted Koppel was covering the story that Mengele might have been found dead in Brazil. And he was going to interview Mengele's son. And there, on TV, was the man I had checked into the motel.

He said, yes, his father was dead, buried in Brazil as had been reported. No, he really didn't know his father. He had been raised by relatives and only met his father a few times. His father was an unrepentant Nazi even then and Rolf wanted little to do with him. Yes, they could exhume the body if they wanted proof. He seemed calm and clearly not thrilled to have to answer questions about a man he barely knew and didn't want to be associated with.

The next day when Rolf came into the lobby to help himself to the complimentary coffee and to check out, I couldn't help staring at him. Is this what the spawn of pure evil looks like? He was less than two years old when World War II ended, so he was hardly responsible for the many sins of his father, but it was hard not to want to say something. To ask him something. What would I say? What was the appropriate response? Among the questions that occurred to me was, why wouldn't you change your name? You have to know people are going to see that name and wonder. To this day, there is a Hitler family in New York who never did, and they are indeed relatives of Dr. Mengele's former Fuhrer. Those are not names I would want to carry. I wouldn't want people looking at me and wondering what my connection was to the most massive crimes against humanity.

He gave me his room key, thanked me, and left. I was left feeling like I had been punched in the gut. I don't know that I have ever stood so near to someone so closely connected to such heinous crimes. Those brief moments with Rolf haunt me still.

My First Close Call in the Business of Hollywood: The Cursed China Doll

I thought I knew something about screenwriting, but quickly found out I didn't. As soon as I established California residency, I started taking a screenwriting class at Santa Monica College. One evening before class, I hit the Burger King across from campus to grab something to eat. Another student from the class happened to be there and asked me to join him. We started talking and somehow got on the topic of what our fathers had done during World War II. My father was in the 14th Air Force, the Flying Tigers, in Kunming, China. His father lied about his age to join the Navy and became a tail gunner on a Dauntless dive bomber in the Pacific.

By the time we had finished our Whoppers, we had outlined on Burger King napkins a screenplay that combined our fathers' stories. It was about a teen who lies about his age to join the Army Air Corps to become a pilot, but instead is assigned to be a mechanic at a repair

The friend with whom I co-wrote China Doll posed in the cockpit of a famous World War II B-17 bomber at an air show in Chino, California that we visited to check out some P-40 fighter planes, the kind featured in our screenplay.

squadron in western China. At the heart of the story is a cursed P-40 airplane that keeps bringing back its dying pilots. No one wants to be assigned that plane. It is number 14. Everyone knows it should have been 13, but the Air Corps was too superstitious to call it that and skipped 13.

The script for what we titled *The China Doll* came together quickly and well. The class and the instructor really liked it and we set about trying to sell it. It was then we began to realize it was the script, not the airplane that was cursed. My co-writer and I were both new to Hollywood and naïve as to how hard it would be to sell a screenplay. We made a few connections and tried to get the script out there.

Someone with contacts to a studio wanted to find some seed money to get the project rolling. He had someone in Las Vegas who might be interested in backing the start-up. We had meetings with the guy in L.A. and phone calls with the guy in Vegas. All was looking good. We were ready to take off. The L.A. guy was going to go to Vegas over a weekend to meet with the money man there, get a check, and we were going to get our airplane script off the ground. But the project crashed and burned before it even taxied onto the runway. The two guys had a big argument. The L.A. guy came back on Monday to tell us the deal was off. He didn't have any other money or sources of money and without that, he couldn't get this rolling. We called the guy in Vegas and he said if we could find another producer, he might be interested, but he had no studio connections, so we were on our own for those. We had no one. Back to the drawing board.

Our next big chance came when my co-writer met the manager of a Star who had just started making a big name for himself when a big career misstep seemed to have derailed his career. He was cast as the almost-naked Star of a movie that made big news, although certainly not big box office nor good reviews. By being seen in so little in the way of clothing in such a bad movie, he was seen as just a dumb piece of hot meat and that reputation made it hard for him to find good parts in Hollywood.

The Star's agent and manager tried to get him roles and kept coming up empty. Their plan changed a bit. He would go to the Middle East and make low-budget sword and sorcery movies, (think: low-budget *Beastmaster*-type flicks), that could still take advantage of his perfect body, keep him acting and making money, and let the bad press in Hollywood die down for a couple of years. He did that and came back to the U.S. looking for the perfect vehicle to relaunch his career. A role that would take advantage of his good looks, but also have some real meat and depth and brains in it to prove he was not just a pretty boy with nothing else to offer.

His manager saw the part of the hot-shot pilot in *China Doll* as the ticket. It was a complex role with a lot of challenges and surprises, but still required the stellar good looks that we described in the script as being a cross between Errol Flynn and Clark Gable. The Star read the script and loved it. He was willing to get his long, flowing locks cut to World War II military length as part of the plan to remake him as someone new. Meeting after meeting followed, usually Friday breakfast meetings at the New World Café in Westwood, near UCLA. Things were rolling along. The manager was able to get interest from people higher up the Hollywood pecking order. A great script with a Star attached. A good package by Hollywood standards. After the last disappointment, we tried not to get our hopes up too much, but it was difficult not to when the Star and the manager both were so excited and pushing so hard to get our script made.

Then came the fateful Friday. The Star came to breakfast alone. We asked where his manager was. He said she would not be coming. He found out that while he was making those movies overseas, she told him he was making a certain amount when in reality, he was making three times more and she was pocketing the difference. He confronted her about it and she seemed blasé. She told him he wasn't complaining while he was making any money. And given how hard it was for him to find roles, he should be grateful that she got him any work at all.

He was far from grateful. He was angry. They had a major blow-up and he told her he would sue her. She told him to forget about it and get his career moving again. He said she owed him a lot of money and an apology. She said that was not going to happen. And if he did take legal action, she'd see to it that he'd never work in this town again. He thought that age-old cliché was just a threat and that she didn't have that kind of power. He called a lawyer. Their relationship was over.

We contacted the manager and she was no longer interested in the project without the Star in the lead. We had several more meetings with the Star. He was not getting his calls returned by agents or managers. Apparently his former manager had put the word out that he was not only tainted as a star, but also was a difficult client. My writing partner went on having Friday breakfasts with the Star for a few months after that, but mainly because he felt sorry for him and let him vent about his bad luck. After a few months, the Star regretted dumping his manager, saying he'd have let her keep the money if he had known the tradeoff was his career.

When I have told this story to people and used the Star's name they invariably say, "Who?" His IMDB page says he has worked a bit since then, but very little, and not for over a decade. Maybe she did have the power to kill his career. Or at least pull the plug on it if he hadn't already put it in a coma by a poor choice early on.

Or maybe it was the script that was cursed. Those two back-to-back setbacks kind of grounded my writing partner and I for a while and although we have occasionally pitched the script since, we have both moved on to other things.

Randy's Donuts in Inglewood, California was popular as much for its giant donut as its delicious breakfast treats. I was lucky enough to catch a cop getting his snack, although he was not happy about having his photo taken.

V.
True Tales from Traffic School

ONE of the many interesting jobs I've had was teaching traffic school. I taught it for over 20 years. I kept track: over 2000 classes, over 50,000 students. I taught as many people how to drive as are in a small city. While living in Venice I drove all of L.A., Orange, Riverside, San Luis Obispo, and Santa Barbara Counties. Once I moved to San Diego, I drove all over that county as well and still made the occasional trek to L.A. for classes up there.

Very few states had traffic schools quite like California's. Many states have traffic school as a last resort: you're about to lose your license. We'll give you one last chance—sometimes with probation, to be reeducated in the law by state officials.

The California schools were run by private companies that had to be licensed and approved by the Department of Motor Vehicles. A few, including California, had "fun" schools. Ones with comedy themes were popular. I worked for a few of those and worked for a comedy-and-magic school for which I had to learn to do a few basic tricks. Other schools had gimmicks to attract students. I worked for a "free pizza" traffic school. There was also a free Chinese food traffic school. There was a school for singles and a gay traffic school. The cleverer or more fun-sounding the name, the more likely students were to pick that school off the list issued by the court.

As instructors, we had to take a very hard test to get licensed. The DMV expected us to know almost everything in the very thick California Vehicle Code. There were several versions of the 100-question test so probably 400 or 500 questions total. Some were so badly worded that even when I knew the answer, I had no idea which answer they wanted. Some questions were so antiquated it was stupid.

One question I remember because I think it was on every version of the test—and I had been warned about it because very few people would know it without advance notice—was, "What is a quadrant?" Sometimes I would stump my traffic school classes with that one. Out of the thousands of people to whom I asked that question, I bet less than five knew the answer. The correct answer was: a gear shift mounted on the steering column of a car—what used to be referred to as "three on the tree." First, second, third, and reverse, to make the four gears of the *quad*-rant. Whenever I thought about those, I thought of a cousin of my grandmother's who had a Plymouth Valiant, from about 1962 that had such a gear shift. As a kid watching him drive made me nervous. I was sure he was going to break his wrist making a turn as he had to reach through the steering wheel to downshift.

Traffic school instructors were required to take the test once every three years for each school that employed us. There were times when I was licensed for as many as five schools which meant I was taking the test more than once a year. Taking it so often almost got me in trouble one time. I was so familiar with the test that I took it too fast. You were allowed one hour for the test so they stamped the time on the back of it. When I took the 100-question test back to the counter 12 minutes after I received it, the DMV clerk wouldn't even grade the test. She was sure I had cheated. She made me wait until she could find someone to watch me take it again, then she gave me a different version of the test that I had to take while an observer sat across from me. I was tempted to race through the test again just to prove I hadn't cheated, but didn't want to deal with the DMV any longer than I had to so I took my time and pretended to puzzle over some answers. I passed, but they didn't seem happy about it. They still seem convinced I had somehow cheated even while being watched. I had learned my lesson, however and in all future tests I took my time and dawdled until I had spent half an hour with the test before I turned it in.

Just getting the traffic school instructor's license the first time presented a challenge for me. I found out I don't have fingerprints. I had to have my fingerprints taken to get the license. And they didn't take. Just little smudges. They tried a few more times. Still not enough to see ridges on the paper. They sent me to another DMV office to have them try, still the ink didn't transfer enough definition from my fingers to the paper to be able to see clear lines. They made some calls and arranged for me to go to a Highway Patrol office in downtown L.A. to have their experts take my fingerprints.

I was not terribly happy with all of the extra driving and time. While I was doing all of this running around, I didn't have a license and couldn't start working. At the CHP office, their expert tried and tried, at times I worried he was going to break a finger, he was pressing them into the paper so hard. While he was doing all of this, we discussed that a few rare people don't have readable prints. Either they were born that way, or certain occupations—such as working around acids, including those found in citrus fruits—and typing a lot can flatten the ridges and make the prints too faint to read. Sometimes even if they could be obtained on paper, there was no way that incidental contact with a surface such as a doorknob would leave a readable print, the way you see them being dusted for in cop shows.

He finally had to admit defeat and had them insert a note in my file saying my prints were unreadable. While I wiped the copious amounts of ink off my fingers, I jokingly said, "I guess this means I can commit all of the crimes I want and you'll never catch me."

Completely deadpan, he looked at me and joked back, "No. What this means is that if we ever come across the scene of a crime and don't find prints, we're coming after you."

Students would often ask how I got started teaching traffic school. "Remember when you were in second grade and the teacher went around the room and asked what you wanted to be when you grew up. Some said 'doctor' some said 'fireman.' A few of us dared to dream big and said, 'traffic school instructor.' And I have lived the dream. I got a B.A. in Traffic Safety from Carnegie Mellon, a Masters in Driving from M.I.T., and a PhD in Advanced Traffic Theory from Stanford…" and usually someone would interrupt and say, "Wow, I had no idea you had to have so much education to teach…" and by then most of the class was cracking up, knowing I was pulling their collective legs.

In reality, all that was required was a high school diploma and passing the test at the DMV I would hang my head and tell the students, "I was once a sinner like yourselves. Then I saw the light. Actually I saw two lights. They were red and blue and flashing." I got a ticket, went to traffic school, and sat there thinking, "I could do this." After class, I talked to the instructor. He said they were hiring. It paid pretty well, was very flexible, and gave me lots of time to write. I applied, got the job.

Even while I was doing other jobs, I kept my hand in teaching traffic school. I enjoyed it and I knew my classes were a lot more fun than the vast majority available out there. I was sought after by other schools so I got paid more than the average instructor. Even when the internet put most schools out of business, I was still teaching a class or three a month until those last few disappeared.

Traffic school was the great equalizer. Everyone got tickets from studio heads and movie stars to musicians to poor immigrants.

Celebrity Offenders

I N my many years of teaching comedy traffic school, especially in the classes in L.A., I had some celebrities in my classes.

One was Jackson Browne. The setting was West L.A. Like many weekday classes, it was mainly older, retired people. In this case, almost all older women, and Jackson. At the beginning of class, I would have everyone tell us their name, what they did for a living, and what their ticket was for. It was a portion of the class that some fellow instructors and I called amongst ourselves, "What's your name and who's your daddy." When we'd talk about our classes, and if something special had happened during that segment, we'd say, "So we were playing 'What's your name and who's your daddy' and this guy says..."

That day during "What's your name and who's your daddy" we got to Jackson Browne and he said his name and, "I'm a singer and songwriter."

And I said, "Yeah, I kinda knew that."

An older woman said, "Do you know him?"

And I said, "Of course. He's Jackson Browne."

Another older woman said, "Who?"

I said, "You know, Jackson Browne. *Running on Empty*."

Another woman asked him, "You got a ticket for running out of gas?"

He and I both laughed. I started listing other of Jackson's hits and these women would shake their heads, "Never heard of it." "Nope." "Don't know it." "Never heard of it."

One woman said, "Oh, wait, I have heard of you! But I thought you were in prison down South somewhere?"

I said, "No, that's James Brown. And he's out now."

It was funny to watch his ego shrink in a roomful of non-fans. He could only laugh it off. He did agree to sing a little of *Lawyers in Love*.

At a break during the class, he told me my class in particular had been recommended to him by Page Hannah, his sort of sister-in-law. At that time, Jackson was living with Page's more famous actress-sister, Daryl. He said my class was living up to how fun Page had said it was.

I was teaching a class in which a woman introduced herself as an actress and I did the standard L.A. joke, "Oh really, what restaurant?" (Most actors in L.A. are more likely waiting tables than starring in movies.) She indignantly replied, "I am not a waitress. I am a very successful actress on a very successful television series!" And the rest of the class was aghast. "Don't you know who that is!?! That's Counselor Troi!" I never watched *Star Trek* so I didn't recognize Marina Sirtis when I met her. She was nice after I apologized. And even more beautiful in person. It was interesting watching the TV series *Picard* many years later and seeing that her character is now married to Commander Riker, played by Jonathan Frakes, whom I've met at Penn State alumni events.

I had a guy in class who said he was an opera singer and I said, "Prove it." And he stood up and did a number from *La Boheme*. I said, "Yeah, okay. You're not faking that."

I had a young Black woman in class who said she was a hip-hop artist. I asked if she'd like to do a little something for us. She said she'd love to, that she was just working out a new number, and she'd like to try it out. She stood up and began performing. There was a 60-something white woman sitting next to her who folded her arms and glared in disgust at the young lady while she performed. When the young lady was done and the applause died out, I asked the older woman, "You didn't enjoy that, did you?"
And she said, "No, I hate that kind of music! I hate hip hop."
"I said, yeah, I kinda figured."
She said, "I'm much more of a rap fan. Actually gangsta rap." And she was serious! She launched into a long rant about how she still misses Tupac and Biggie and how Snoop's later stuff isn't nearly as good as his earlier stuff...she knew her rap. She and the Black woman went out for lunch together to discuss music. Go figure. I thought hip hop was too wild for her tastes. It was too mild.

Speaking of misjudging people's musical tastes...I had a class in which a student said he was a corporate attorney and a major in the Marine Corps Reserves. He had the regulation Marine haircut and sort of sat at attention during the class. It was easy to picture him as a rigid drill instructor. We all scattered for lunch break and we returned, the lawyer came into the room sobbing. We asked what was wrong. He could barely stammer out, "Jerry Garcia died. I just heard Jerry Garcia died."
We asked if he knew Jerry and he said, "No, but I feel like I did. I've seen *The Dead* 78 times. I've flown all over the country to see them perform."
We all took turns comforting him on his loss, but I could tell we were all wondering how well this Marine/lawyer would fit in among the Deadheads at a concert. But we shouldn't stereotype.

I was teaching at the Comedy Store in La Jolla, which has a piano next to the stage. In class one day, I had one of the big names of country music. I don't follow country, so I can't remember who it was—Jimmy Bob Ray Joe Eddie Dan—one of those names. A lot of big celebrities who want to escape Hollywood have places in the San Diego suburbs of La Jolla or Rancho Santa Fe, so I was not that surprised when I'd have celebrities in class. About half the class knew who this singer was and the other half, like me, did not. Those who knew were very impressed. It was one of the few times I ever saw anyone ask for an autograph in class.

I asked our star if he'd like to sing something for us. He said sure and asked if he could use the piano. He came up and started improvising the *Traffic School Blues*. It was amazing, verse after verse of hilarious lyrics with great blues and jazz riffs on the piano between verses while he thought up the next part. I couldn't believe the talent he had to be coaxing such great music out of that old piano while making up funny rhymes on the spot. When he was done, he got a huge round of applause. I told him how incredible it was and said I wished we could have recorded it. And he said, "So do I! There was some really good stuff in there, wasn't there! I would have liked to capture that!"

One of our other instructors, Craig, had the then-president of Sony Pictures in one of his classes. I won't embarrass the guy by using his name. As a wannabe actor, Craig recognized the man right away. The guy had been in the news recently because Sony had bumped his pay to something like $200M a year (before perks and bonuses). Craig said to him, "Meaning no disrespect, but can't you afford the ticket?" The man said, yes, but he had received so many tickets that one more ding on his record and he'd lose his license. Craig said, "Meaning no disrespect, but can't you afford a chauffeur?" The man said, yes, but there are times when you want to be alone for a drive or with just one other person so he wanted to keep his license. He said he called his lawyer and asked him what he should do. His lawyer replied, "Go to traffic school." The guy said, "That's what it says in the court paper. I could've figured that out. If that's all you're going to tell me, why am I calling you?" His lawyer replied, "I don't know. You just wasted another $600."

Another good Craig story (not celebrity-related). Craig was from the Cayman Islands and like many people from the Caribbean, he was of mixed African, Spanish, English, and other heritage. Depending on how Craig dressed, fixed his hair, wore earrings, et cetera, he could look Black or Latino or white. Back then LAPD still had a place on their ticket form for "race" and when Craig himself got pulled over once, he said the cop kept looking at him and looking at him and finally asked, "What race are you?" Craig answered, "What race do I have to be to not get the ticket?" The police officer was not amused. Craig got the ticket.

A non-celebrity, non-entertaining story...

I had a young man in class who, when I asked what he did, answered that he worked at Subway, but he really was a musician. He said, "I'm actually a bit of a guitar virtuoso. I'm in the same league with Eric Clapton and Eddie Van Halen, really."

I said, "Wow. That is impressive. I'd love to hear you play."

He said, "Yeah, too bad we don't have a guitar." I went to my boss's office, knowing he kept his guitar in there, brought it out and handed it to the kid.

He took it in his hands and looked at it. He swallowed hard and looked up at me very sheepishly. "Uh, uh, you have a guitar."

I said yes and that we were all eager to hear him play.

He swallowed again then looked at the guitar again and moved his hands around a little on it. Then looked back at me and said, "This is a guitar. You have a guitar."

I said yes. I asked what he'd like to play.

He ran his hand down the neck of it again then looked back at me and said, very quietly, "I don't know how to play the guitar."

I could tell he just wanted the floor to open and swallow him, he was so humiliated. I took the guitar back into the office while the rest of the class, the ones who couldn't hear what he had said, just looked on in puzzlement.

At the next break in the class a man came up to me and said, "That was really cruel the way you embarrassed that kid." And I said, "I didn't embarrass him! I really thought we were all in for a huge treat the way he bragged he could play. He embarrassed himself."

I doubt that kid has done much boasting about his musical abilities since.

A Village in Botswana Gets a Doctor

ONE of the most moving traffic school moments was when my class inspired a man from Botswana to finish medical school.

I really did try to have fun with my classes and wanted to make sure they had a good time. If I ever felt one of my lectures becoming too serious, to lighten things up, I would interrupt myself saying, "Okay, sermon is over. Let us all now turn to page 42 in our hymnals and sing *A Mighty Fortress is my Dodge*."

By the eighth hour of the class, no matter how fun it had been, people were getting antsy and I wanted them to leave in a good mood, so after they had filled out the certificates which they would have to file with the court as proof of having completed the class, and I had signed them, I would say, "Okay, just one more thing..." and watch them tense up knowing the class wasn't quite over. And I would hit the button on my cassette player to start playing *Pomp and Circumstance* indicating it was graduation time. It always got a laugh and was a fun way to wrap up the day. I'd ask if anyone had their parents waiting outside to come in to take photos and if they all had their caps and gowns ready to put on.

Then I would give out class awards based on how people had acted in class, the stories they had told, and their offenses. As I gave each person their certificate, I'd name someone valedictorian, say someone was voted "Most likely to get a DUI," "Most likely to do jail time for a traffic offense," "Most likely to appear on *Cops*", "Most likely to be back soon," and similar jokes that given the personalities in the room, would get laughs.

Without even giving it much thought, when we got to the young man from Botswana who said he was a med student at UCLA, I named him, "Most likely to succeed." And a remarkable thing happened. The class burst out in applause and cheering. They had laughed at the other jokes, but without any prompting, they cheered for this guy.

When they were done applauding, he said, "May I say something?" I said of course and the class nodded in agreement. He said, "Last night, I told you I was here studying medicine in UCLA. But I didn't tell you the whole story. I am on a U.N. grant that only pays my most basic expenses. Tuition, books and a small stipend toward room and board. I have no spending money. My village—and it is a very poor village—takes up a collection every month to send me $50 so that I can buy any other essentials I need—toothpaste, shampoo, clothes. Every once in a while, I treat myself to a $1 hamburger at McDonald's, but that is the only time I eat out. I have been miserable since I have been here. I have no friends. I don't fit in with the white students, I don't fit in with the black students. A few times when I first got here, people did ask me to join them for lunch or to go out for a drink after class, but I can't afford things like that and had to say no and they stopped asking.

I am so lonely. Los Angeles is a very big, cold, unfriendly place. I have been so unhappy here. All the money this ticket cost me is going to set me back financially for months and I decided to give up. I have spent the last few days working on a letter to my mother telling her I am coming home. I can't take this anymore. I know she will be very disappointed and I know I will be letting down my village. They have worked so hard to help me be here. The letter is so hard to write. Trying to express how bad I feel. Then, something amazing happened last night. I came to this class. And everyone was so nice. More people talked to me in this class than in all of my classes at UCLA. And you, sir!" He pointed to a guy on the far side of the room. "You don't know what you did for me last night."

The guy looked surprised and shrugged like, what did I do? The med student continued. "Last night we went down to the convenience store and I put my soda and candy bar on the counter while I counted out coins. I knew I shouldn't waste money on a Coke and Snickers, but I just need to do something for myself now and then. I especially needed that little bit of cheering up now as I write the most difficult letter of my life. And while I was looking at my few coins, debating if I should really spend the money, you slid my candy and Coke can with your stuff to the clerk and said to me, 'Don't worry. I've got it.' Like it was no big thing. But it was, it was a big thing. No one has given me anything since I have been in this city. I was so touched, I wanted to save that Snickers bar, it meant so much to me and you barely let me even thank you."

He went on, "And then tonight, you all cheered for me. You all really cheered for me. He told me I'd succeed. No one has done that since I have been here. You proved there are caring people in this city. It gave me hope that some people believe in me. It gave me such hope that I might meet good people here. That I might be able to do this and make it and go back and serve my village. I want to tear up that letter and try to stay and become a doctor."

We were all wiping away tears. And then another amazing thing happened. It started with the guy who bought him a Snickers bar. The man got up, walked over to the med student, and dropped two $20 bills on the table in front of him and said, "Take yourself out to eat." The woman sitting next to the med student opened her purse and slid money to him. Then someone else got up and handed him some money. Even me, broke as I was, kicked in some money. No one counted it, but by the time the class was done, the guy probably had $200 or more on the table in front of him and everyone was openly crying. Some village in Africa might have a doctor because of us!

More Snapshots of Traffic School...

WHEN I was teaching a lot, I got good at flushing my memory of the class as soon as it was over. There were too many people to try to remember and the classes and students—with rare exceptions—all began to look alike after a while. The only ones I remembered were because there was something special about them, good or bad.

I even had drivers in cars next to me at a red light tap their horn, roll down the window and yell, "Traffic school! See! I stopped behind the limit line!" I ran into former students at the airport and at theaters. Perhaps the craziest encounter was during the 1992 Olympics when I was walking down Las Ramblas in Barcelona and heard someone yell, "Yo! Traffic school dude!" I was thinking: I can't even go to Spain and get away from it.

When I would run into former students on the street or in a store, they would often be offended that I didn't recognize them. They were each sure I found them so special I would still remember them even years after they were in my class.

One afternoon I went right from class to the gym. I changed clothes and plopped right down, and started doing sit-ups as part of my warmup routine. A woman got down next to me, started doing sit-ups, and chatting with me. She was talking with such an easy familiarity that it struck me as odd behavior for a stranger at the gym and I finally said, "I'm sorry, do I know you?" She got a hurt look on her face and said, "I was in your traffic school class until..." she checked her watch, "... about 20 minutes ago." I said I was sorry, but out of context, in different clothes...

One evening I ran into a guy at the grocery store. It started as a typical interaction with a former student. He stopped me in the produce section and smiled, "Traffic school!" I smiled back and gave him my standard response (whether I remembered them or not, and I usually did not), "Hey, good to see you! Are you behaving yourself?"

He said he was and then started talking about some crazy guy who had been in the class with him. I nodded politely. He went on about the nutcase and I nodded. And he said, "You don't remember this class?"

I had to admit I did not. He said, "It was the one with the musician and the actor," as though that would narrow it right down in Southern California. It would be much easier to remember the rare class that didn't have a musician and an actor.

He told me some more about the bizarre behavior of his fellow student and said, "I can't believe you don't remember this class! I've told that story like 20 times! I tell it to everyone I meet! I have never had to deal at close range for eight hours with anyone so crazy! I can't believe you don't remember him!"

I replied, "Sir, even if he did everything you said he did—and I am not questioning your word—he doesn't even warrant honorable mention of the craziest people I've had in traffic school. He wouldn't even make the top 25 craziest people I've had in class."

He walked away stunned. And I thought, how crazy was it that I had met so many crazy students that I had no recollection of the one he was talking about.

The woman in a traffic school class in San Diego was wearing a straw hat with a brim that stuck out almost three feet all the way around. Every time she moved, she was swatting someone nearby with it. I suggested that out of deference to her fellow students, she might want to remove the hat. She said, as her eyes sort of rolled around in their sockets, "Good lord, no! Do you know what fluorescent lights do to your brain?" It was at this point I noticed the dome of the hat was lined on the inside with aluminum foil. I had never seen that in real life before, only as a joke on television.

When it came time for me to ask what her ticket was for, she said, "I don't know."

I said, "What do you mean, you don't know?"

"I don't know." She said, "Everyone else has stuff. If I got a ticket would I have stuff?"

I asked, "Stuff?"

She took the papers from the man next to her and held them up. "Stuff. He has stuff." And pointing around she said, "And she has stuff, and he has stuff. Everyone else seems to have stuff. I don't have stuff."

I explained that that was the paperwork the court mailed out when they got their tickets. I borrowed the ticket someone had with them and showed it to her and said, "Or, some people brought their actual tickets. Did you get something like this? Could also be blue or yellow?" She didn't seem to recognize a ticket. I asked, "Did a police officer pull you over and give you one of these?"

"I don't think so. I don't remember. But I don't have stuff."

"You would probably remember if you got a ticket. It is kind of a big deal for most people. And then, yes the court would have mailed you stuff."

"I don't have stuff. So maybe I should leave now?"

"Maybe you should. If you find your stuff and want to come back, give the school a call okay?"

And she left. She sat in a traffic school class where she apparently didn't have to be and then she left. How or why she found the class, I couldn't guess. I just hoped the hat didn't block her vision while she was driving.

When I was teaching a class in West L.A. and asked a man his occupation, he answered that he was an astrologer. In reaction to my reaction he said, "Sure, go ahead and roll your eyes. Libras almost never buy into astrology." Again, noting my reaction, he said, "See? You are a Libra, aren't you? In fact, you are so thoroughly a Libra that I would bet one...no...I would bet *both* your parents are Libras, aren't they?" Again, noting my expression he said, "I thought so! I can always tell people's signs."

He then talked about each person who had already introduced themselves and based on the few moments they had spoken, he guessed their sign. "That guy is a Taurus. Even sits like a Taurus. She's an Aries. Gotta be an Aries. Oh, and that woman is a Gemini. Only a Gemini would want to sit next to another Gemini. That guy even walks like a Scorpio!" And so on, all around the room. Of the more than 30 people he talked about, he was only wrong on one and that woman said if she had been born 12 hours earlier she would have been the sign he guessed, but her mother had an exceptionally long labor.

The astrologer smiled smugly. It did make us all wonder.

One April 15th, a student introduced himself as a tax accountant. I said, "Do you know what day it is? Shouldn't you be doing somebody's taxes?" He said, "Yes, but I already got two extensions on this ticket and they wouldn't give me a third and it's due tomorrow. So I'm going to finish class then run back to the office and finish a few more tax returns. Then race them to the post office." He jokingly added, "And probably get another ticket."

The man next to him said, "Why bother? I don't do taxes."

The accountant said, "Lots of people don't do taxes. That's why they hire me. They bring me shoeboxes full of receipts and..."

"No, you don't get it. I don't do taxes. I'm not going to fill out their silly forms and sweat out every April 15th, the way everybody else in this stupid country does."

"But you have to..."

"No, I don't. I figure they can keep whatever they kept, but I'm not going to jump their silly hoops and worry about it. I just don't file anything."

The tax guy was incredulous, "But..."

"The IRS are idiots. I figured out the system. If you never file a tax return, they aren't expecting one next year so they don't even know to look for one." He added, smugly, "I've been working, I dunno 30, 35 years and I have never filed a tax return ever. And I've never gotten in trouble and I've never heard a peep from them."

"But if they ever do find out..."

"They're never going to find out. I'm telling ya, they're stupid."

All I could say was, "Wow." And I moved on to talk to the next person in class and asked him what his name was and what he did for a living. He said, "My name is Michael and I am a field auditor for the Internal Revenue Service of the United State Government." The whole class laughed. It was a very funny line. I said, "Seriously, what do you do?" Completely serious, he replied, "I am a field auditor for the Internal Revenue Service and..." turning to the tax scofflaw he said, "And you, sir, are in a lot of trouble." He pulled out a business card and handed it to the man saying, "You may want to call me and set up a time to come in. That will be easier and go better for you than if we have to track you down."

The man's eyes bulged as he looked at the card in his hand and realized that the IRS agent wasn't joking. The rest of the class stopped laughing and it got very, very quiet.

The closest restaurant to the motel conference room where one of my classes was held was a good Mexican place, and often a large number of students would go there for lunch. One day 12 or 15 of us went there and had nice meal. On the way out, many of us grabbed a mint or two from the large dish on the hostess' stand. One of the students from the class unzipped her large purse, picked up the entire bowl and dumped it in her purse as the rest of us watched in shock. I'm sure none of us had ever seen this before. The dish held hundreds of mints. It was big enough that it could have held half a basketball.

As strange as it was to watch, no one said anything. What could we say? I was certainly speechless. We returned to class, people, including me, who had managed to get a mint before she took them all, were opening our mints and popping them in their mouths. Seeing this, one man said, "I should have gotten a mint." He turned to the woman with the purse-load of them and asked her for one. That's when things got really weird. She said, "Why would you ask me? I don't have any." All of us who had watched her fill her purse blinked and let out an involuntary collective, "Huh?"

He said to her, "Obviously, you don't have to give me a mint, but given that you have a purseful of them, I thought you might share."

She said, "I don't know what you're talking about."

The man looked around at his fellow lunchmates for some sort of corroboration and we all nodded that we indeed had witnessed the same thing he had. We could all see her bulging bag sitting in front of her. Noticing where we were all looking, she moved her purse to the floor.

I should note that there was nothing odd about this woman's behavior through the first half of the class and she was quite pleasant and normal and social at lunch. She sat next to the man who now wanted a mint and there was nothing about her demeanor to have led him to believe she'd deny him. He was getting a little irked and said, "I know you don't have to give me a mint, but you do have a whole bag of them."

She said, "I do not."

I said, "Obviously I can't compel you to give him a mint, but why don't you open your purse and show him you don't have any?"

She was now becoming indignant. "I don't have any mints and I don't have to open my purse!"

Another woman said, "True, you don't have to open your purse, but we all saw you dump an entire bowl of mints in there. How can you deny it?"

She said, "I don't know what you're talking about!"

A few other people tried to goad her into opening her purse or sharing, but with no success. We resumed class still puzzling over her behavior. I don't know if she had some sort of kleptomania where she honestly didn't remember taking the mints or what, but it was strange.

I prided myself on making my classes fun and interesting, which wasn't easy given how people were conditioned to hate traffic school and were often still bitter about the whole ticketing process, from getting pulled over to the red tape of the courts. Plus the fines and fees that kept increasing.

Most people showed up in a bad mood, or at best in a neutral mood. I liked the classes where within a half an hour so, I had them laughing and realizing it wasn't going to be so bad. Sometimes it took a few hours to loosen them up. One of my fellow instructors said that during that slog through the warm-up period, she often found herself thinking, "Could we just skip ahead to the part where you're having a good time and you think the class is amusing?" It was often work to break the ice.

Sometimes there would be one student who refused to give in and enjoy themselves no matter what. Sometimes I would see them suppressing a smile, but they were determined to try to maintain their pout. Even if it took all day, I took it as a challenge to bring them around and when they did finally laugh, I relished the victory. Sometimes that person would come up after class and apologize and say they should have relaxed sooner. But sometimes they left as bitter and angry as they came. A few stories of those "problem children" as we used to call them:

I was having a great class on a Saturday in Mission Valley. They were laughing and participating and having a good time. All except for that woman in the corner who kept her arms folded, and even with her dark glasses on, I could tell the eyes I couldn't see were scowling. I tried every trick I knew to engage her, but nothing was working. At some point after lunch I gave up, thinking, to hell with you, you miserable *&%$. Class ended and everyone left, but her. I was sure this was going to be when she told me how offensive my jokes were, how bad a teacher I was, and the general rant I had heard a few times over my many years of teaching. Not often, but even a half a dozen such conversations were painfully memorable.

Instead, she took off her glasses and I could see her eyes were red from crying. She said, "I just wanted to say thank you for a wonderful day. You are really talented and funny. Today was a great distraction for me. I had a good time."

She could see the startled look on my face as I said, "You didn't seem to be having a good time."

She said, "I know. And I'm sorry about that. I know you were trying to make me laugh, and that is why I stayed to talk to you, but…"

She hesitated until she got the lump in her throat under control and said, "I wasn't sure I should come today. I almost cancelled. I just buried my mother on Thursday. I didn't want to be here, but I thought if I stay home I'll just be stewing in my grief, traffic school is going to suck anyway, I might as well get it over with. But you were great. I really did enjoy it. I'm not at the place where I can laugh or smile yet, but yours was a nice distraction, so thank you."

I went from thinking she was a miserable *&%$ to hugging her goodbye. Good lesson in not judging what is going on in people's heads. As the old saying goes, "be kind, for everyone you meet is fighting a great battle you know nothing about."

There was a nasty man at another class at a different location in Mission Valley. One of those rare jerks I had in class who wanted everyone else to be as miserable as they were. He tried a few times to disrupt the class and I had to threaten to eject him, minus the certificate he needed for court. In every class I did my graduation ceremony with *Pomp and Circumstance*, and everyone always stayed until all of the other students got their certificates. He did not. He grabbed his papers and bolted from the room. We could hear his old clunker pickup truck fire up in the parking lot and rubber squeal as he pulled out. I went to the window and looked out, as did a few other students, and we watched as he drove his truck through the hedges, over the lawn and out of the parking lot.

The owner of the school called him the next day and told him that we had already called the court and put a hold on his certificate. If he didn't pay for the damages, he not only wouldn't get credit for class, but we'd have him arrested. The stupidity of it was staggering. We had all of his information from him registering for the class: driver's license number, address, phone number, and more. He paid for the damages.

Then there was the very unhappy young lady in a Saturday class. She was about 24 years old. And she was angry. The hostility was just rising off her throughout the class like heat off a July sidewalk. It's cliché to say, "if looks could kill," but every time I looked at her the enmity was so palpable it almost derailed my train of thought. When I wasn't looking at her, I could still feel her loathing.

I did something I had only done once or twice in all of my classes. I didn't ask her to introduce herself or talk about her ticket until the very end. We always filled out certificates last, and I even waited until after we had done that to address her. I didn't want to pull the pin on that grenade any sooner because if it blew up in my face, I didn't want to live with the fallout any longer than I had to. Finally, I summoned my courage and said, "Hi. What's your name?"

She said, "Fuck you."

I said, "I beg your pardon?"

She said, "You heard me. Fuck you."

I said, "I did hear you. I just couldn't believe you really said that."

"What's so hard to believe? You suck. Traffic school sucks. The cops suck. This ticket sucks. Fuck you."

I said, "Okay. From the way you have been sitting there all day, all coiled up and angry, that was pretty much the reaction I was anticipating that is why I waited until the last minute to go there. And that is fine, you don't have to talk, but before we leave I would just like to say, I hope for your sake that you never really have a major crisis in your life, because if getting a traffic ticket derails your little trolley this badly..."

She stood up, gave me the finger, said, "Fuck you!" again and stormed out. The rest of the class just kind of looked at each other in sad puzzlement. After the class ended, I half expected her to come back and demand her certificate. I was not looking forward to that confrontation if she did, but luckily she didn't.

On Monday I called the owner of the school to tell him what happened. At every school for which I worked, the owners or managers always wanted to be forewarned if they might be getting a complaint from a student. And from a selfish standpoint, it was always good for them to have heard my side of it first. I told him what happened, and I said, "And she is probably going to call and say I was a dick, and demand her money back with her certificate." I told him he could call anyone else in the class and ask them what happened. "I handled it as best I could and to be technical, she didn't complete the required eight hours of class—there was still ten minutes left when she bolted so she has yet to complete the class."

I checked back a few days later and she hadn't called. When that traffic school closed down about a year later, her certificate was still in the drawer, unclaimed, with a note clipped to it. She had wasted seven hours and 50 minutes in my class, paid the $40, and had nothing to show for it. I'm sure that just added to her anger at the whole thing. I wondered if she had let the anger build up until she had a stroke. I was curious what happened to her in her young life that she was so twisted up over this ticket. I felt sorry for her and I hope she found a way to deal with her issues before they killed her.

At some point the traffic offenses became a blur. Often when I would tell a friend that I had a celebrity in my class they'd ask, "Oh, what did he do?" The minor speeding, running red lights and stops signs all became meaningless to me. There were, however, a few offenses that stand out in memory.

One guy, whose IQ was probably not much bigger than his shoe size, when asked him what his ticket was for answered, "I don't know."

I asked, "Didn't the cop tell you?"

"He wasn't making any sense."

"May I see your ticket?" By this point I had learned the vehicle code section numbers for all the common offenses. I read it and said, "You were charged with making an illegal U-turn."

"That's what the cop seemed to be saying, but I didn't."

"Well, what happened?"

"I was driving down Downey Boulevard, and as I'm getting up to the light, I see there is a 'No U-turn' sign but I want to be going the other way, so I made a U-turn there. Before the intersection."

I said, "Doesn't that part of Downey Boulevard have a wide median, with like a planter down the middle?"

"Yeah."

"And you made a U-turn *over* the planter???"

"Yeah. It wasn't posted."

"You made a U-turn OVER the planter!!!"

"It wasn't posted. It was posted at the intersection and I didn't make one there. If they didn't want me doing one, they should have posted it."

"I would have thought building a foot-high wall and planting petunias would have been sufficient discouragement for most people."

"My truck is kinda raised up so..."

Clearly I was not going to have any more success than the cop did at explaining what was wrong with his driving.

Then there was the guy who made what could perhaps best be described as a Q-turn on the 405 Freeway. The guy said he didn't even want to go to his wife's stupid nephew's wedding and then she takes forever getting ready, "So we're already 20 minutes late leaving, and, as usual, she expects me to make it up in drive time. And she is so busy bitching at me, she didn't tell me to get off at the Westwood exit. Then she tells me, 'You missed the exit.' I am *not* going to listen to her bitch for another exit, get off at Sunset, have to come back around, so I swung over to the right lane and made a U-turn back to the left lane and zipped down until I was below Westwood, then zipped across and took the exit."

I was dumbfounded. "You drove against traffic on the 405 Freeway?!?"

"Yeah. It was a Saturday afternoon. There wasn't much traffic."

<Dear reader, I must take a step back from my narrative to ask you if you have ever driven in Los Angeles, and if you have that it might be remotely possible that there could be a Saturday afternoon with little to no traffic on the 405 in Westwood. If you have never been to L.A. and need to phone a friend who has, please do. I'll wait.>

The CHP pulled him over and took his license on the spot. His attendance at 16 hours of traffic school was part of his plea bargain that included a license suspension, and a large fine.

Then there was the guy who got a ticket for cooking while driving. Technically the charge was "distracted driving" or something vague like that. He said he had a long commute and he didn't like to "waste time," so he cooked and ate his breakfast on the way to work and cooked and ate dinner on the way home. I said, "What do you mean you cook dinner in your car?"

He said he had taken out the right front passenger seat in his Toyota Celica and put in a kitchen: a dorm-sized refrigerator and on top of that he had mounted a blender. He had a hot pot on a gyro pivot like you might see on a boat to avoid sloshing hot coffee or soup or oatmeal, if he had to stop quickly.

I said I was surprised a car battery could power all of that. He said, "I learned the hard way, it can't. I had to redo the car's electrical system and load the trunk with RV batteries."

He was so proud of this that at the break he took anyone who was interested on a field trip to his car. Sure enough it was as he described. He opened the fridge. He had eggs and bacon and milk for the next day's breakfast and he had pork chops for dinner.

He had spent so much time and effort reconfiguring his car that when his engine or transmission would give out, he'd replace them rather than try to recreate the kitchen. He had such a long commute, he drove over 50,000 miles a year, so even a Toyota would only last a half-dozen years at that level of driving.

Everyone was looking at him as though he was crazy, but he was sure he was a genius and wondered why everyone didn't commute this way. He said the cop tried to find a section of the vehicle code that prohibited a kitchen in the passenger compartment, but couldn't find one and had to settle for citing the guy for distracted driving and warning him to not do it again. From how well-stocked the refrigerator and pantry were, I don't think he listened.

Which brings to mind another "only in L.A." traffic moment. I was on a crowded freeway in what truckers sometimes call slinky traffic, where the traffic slows down abruptly and bunches up, then speeds up to 40 or 50 and spreads out, only to have to slam on the breaks again. And I kept hearing trumpet music. And I was thinking, "Wow, that person has a great stereo. That trumpet sounds so real and close..."

And then the next lane caught up with mine again and I looked over. A man in the car next to me was playing the trumpet, steering with his knees. Driving in L.A. made me nervous.

Then there was the traffic school student who said he'd always had bad luck with police. He told us a story unrelated to the ticket that brought him to class. He said he was a photographer and at one point in his career he had been hired to shoot the official portrait of the Mayor of Detroit. When he arrived at City Hall, he couldn't find parking anywhere nearby. He drove around the block several times in a widening circle and still couldn't find anything so he decided he'd unload his equipment in front of the building, run it in, then move his car, even if it meant parking blocks away. He had stopped at a red curb with his flashers on and was about to start unloading, when a cop came up and said, "You can't park here."

The photographer replied, "I'm not parking. I'll only be a minute. I'm just here to shoot the Mayor."

A few hours later, after he was released from jail, parking was no longer a problem, as his car had been impounded to be searched.

Speaking of red curbs, when I would teach my classes about curb colors, I would say, "What does a blue curb mean?" A few students would guess "handicapped parking" and I would say, "No, Smurf parking only." And when I got to a white curb, I would ask what it meant and people would answer, "passenger loading." And I would say, "No, only white people can park there." I had Black and brown people literally fall out of their chairs laughing at that line. And I thought it was funny that the white students had to look around to see if the people of color were laughing before they sort of had permission to laugh before they joined in. I had a few Black people say that was their favorite line in the entire class and were surprised I was brave enough to use it. But no one ever complained.

And speaking of accommodations for the disabled, I would often ask my classes if it was illegal to ride a skateboard on a sidewalk. Most people thought it was. And I would say, "No, it's not. If it were illegal, do you think they would have lowered the curbs at intersections and put those ramps in for them. And invariably someone would say, "Those are for wheelchairs." And I'd reply, "Don't be ridiculous. People in wheelchairs can't ride skateboards." And the class would howl with laughter. I loved setting the class up to set me up.

When I talked about parking for the handicapped, I would say it was not up to the average citizen to enforce those restrictions. I had many disabled people say they were often confronted because they "didn't look handicapped." "Hey, I don't see your cane or wheelchair! Why do you people get to park there? You look fine to me." I would explain that people with heart or lung conditions that prohibited them from walking long distances might also qualify for a placard and it wasn't up to other drivers to judge.

I had a veteran in class who said he lost a leg in the Vietnam War. I couldn't tell from the way he walked or sat that there was anything wrong with him and he said lots of other people couldn't either because he often was confronted about his use of handicapped parking. I didn't realize that phantom pain went on forever. He said even after all these years, the leg that wasn't there still hurt. And he said the worst was the itching. The bottom of his foot that wasn't there itched often. He could scratch the plastic all day and it's not going to stop. He said he'd had a bad night when his foot was really itching and he hadn't slept and was already really cranky. The next morning, he parked in the blue space in front of his bank and a man stepped in front of him and said, "Hey, what are you doing parking there? You look fine. I don't see anything wrong with you. You're not handicapped!" He said he wasn't in the mood to deal with such rudeness so he reached down and through his pant leg unbuckled the harness and let the prosthetic leg drop out. He glared at the man and demanded, "Now am I handicapped enough to park here?" The man nervously nodded. The guy said, "Good. Now if you'll hand me my leg, I'll go do my banking. Thank you."

I had a woman in her late 20s arrive in class in a wheelchair. She was not in good humor and it was not because of her ticket. She had just parked in the handicapped spot at the building that housed the traffic school and a few other businesses, including a veterinarian. The young lady said that when she parked in the blue spot, an older woman stopped and started berating her. "You know those spots are for the elderly! Young people like you shouldn't be using those!"

The young lady said she was used to this reaction, and if people only saw this young person sitting in the car it was somewhat understandable. But in many cases the person giving her the lecture didn't let up when they saw her wheelchair. And that was the case this morning. She had already pulled the wheelchair out of the backseat and was preparing to do her swing over from the driver's seat into the chair when she was accosted by the woman and "her yappy little dog." The young lady did not have legs. Her need for a wheelchair seemed pretty self-evident. She said the entire way up the long and winding ramp the older woman continued to yell at her. The young lady said to her, "If I don't qualify for a handicapped placard, who does? Do you have to be dead?"

Later in the class when I asked her what she did for a living she said she was a professional pool player. When she wasn't playing in tournaments, she hustled pool in a billiard parlor near San Diego State University. I asked, "Guys play you for money?"

She said, "Oh yeah!"

I said, "Meaning no disrespect, but if you challenged me to play for money, I'd assume you've got game and not go anywhere near that."

She laughed. "These young guys, in front of their friends, their egos on the line...they're not going to lose to some dainty little Asian chick in a wheelchair. They're the ones who want to bet. I just go along. Then I mop the table with them."

A few months later, I happened to catch a few minutes of a pool tournament on *Wide World of Sports* and there she was playing for $50,000 at a tournament in Las Vegas.

Another interesting person I had in class was Mark Goffeney. I'll use Mark's real name since he is somewhat of a local legend, having played music around San Diego for years. He has even done standup comedy.

Mark doesn't have arms. He learned to drive a car, as he does everything else, with his feet. It was rather fascinating to watch him balance on one leg while he pulled out his wallet with the other foot, open the wallet and count out bills with his toes. His toes are more dexterous than my fingers. I certainly can't play the guitar as well as he does with any of my appendages. Mark has long hair and looks like a bit of a hippy, so sometimes he'd get hassled by police. He told us that one day he got pulled over and the cop approached the car with his gun drawn and ordered Mark to stick his hands out the window. Mark said, "I was tempted to tell the cop I was unarmed, but I wasn't sure he'd get the joke." Instead he yelled back that he'd comply, but he didn't have arms. The cop was getting angrier, "Then how are you driving, smartass!"

There are lots of videos online of Mark playing guitar, often busking in Balboa Park. He said he loved reading the comments on YouTube: "You can tell it's fake." "His arms are pinned behind him." "It's photoshopped." As though playing a guitar with your toes wouldn't still be a talent even if you had arms. I still see Mark out playing guitar in the park or elsewhere around town or run into him at the coffee shop we both frequent and we always say hi.

Anne was probably in her late 20s. She said she had been fixed up on a date by a mutual friend. The guy wanted to see her again, but she thought he was a bit of a jerk and said no. A few weeks later, the mutual friend called and said, "Jason knows you don't want to go on another date, but he has his company's Christmas party coming up and thinks it will look bad if he can't get a date. Would you go with him? Not as a date, he knows it won't be that. You'd just be his escort. He knows you'd make a good impression on his boss. Please do it as a favor to me." After some cajoling and the promise of a nice dinner out, she agreed to do it for her friend.

It was a decision she was to regret as she was to find out just how big a jerk he was. Her friend felt so bad about what happened, she was paying for part of the thousands of dollars that evening out had cost.

At the holiday party, Jason rapidly got drunk and decided it was a good idea to tell his boss exactly what he thought of him. Jason was fired before the dancing started. She and a few of Jason's now-former coworkers steered him to the door before he could start any more trouble, which given his drunken belligerence, seemed likely.

Anne was already arguing with Jason about his driving, given his condition, when to her grateful surprise, the valet refused to give Jason his keys. Seeing Jason shouldn't be behind the wheel, the valet gave them to her and suggested she drive. There was more of an argument, but when the valet made it clear he was not going to let Jason into the driver's seat of the BMW, she got in.

Anne said she limits herself to one glass of wine if she is driving, but when the evening started she didn't know she'd be driving home and, as Jason became more embarrassingly drunk she was drinking to relax in the face of his bad behavior. Then she cut herself off, thinking she might have to call a cab or find her own way home and didn't want to be too impaired to do that.

She said she considered a moment before getting in the BMW. Was she okay to drive? She felt okay and took a quick inventory. She knew she was likely over the legal limit, but she felt fine.

Driving down the 405 Freeway, Jason announced that he needed to pee. Anne said, "Fine, I'll take the next exit and we'll find a McDonald's or whatever."

He said, "No, that's ok. No need to stop." He opened the sunroof on his Beemer. She asked what the hell thought he was doing? He told her not to worry, he had done this before. He undid his seatbelt, stood on the seat projecting himself out the sunroof, and started unzipping his pants. She yelled at him to sit down. He could not seriously be thinking about relieving himself on the freeway! She started yanking on his pant leg in an attempt to get him to sit down. With her eyes and one hand on him, she apparently began weaving. That is when the red and blue lights started flashing in the mirror.

She pulled over. She didn't doubt that her breath smelled like wine. Or that she had been swerving. She flunked the field sobriety test, she said likely more out of anger than inebriation. The CHP officers gave her a breathalyzer. She was over the state's legal limit for driving, not a lot, but definitely over, which she didn't doubt given the wine. As one officer started placing her under arrest, the other officer handed the keys to Jason saying, "The little lady here has had too much to drink. I guess you'll have to take her BMW home for her."

Anne said she lost it. As they handcuffed her, she yelled at the cops, "Are you fucking kidding me? The only reason I was driving *his* car is that he is clearly too drunk to drive! He was trying to piss out the sunroof of a BMW on the freeway for fuck's sake! If that doesn't say 'drunk' I don't know what does! You can't let him drive!"

She said if she had any chance of convincing the officers she hadn't had too much to drink, her tirade blew her chances of that because she was beyond livid. As they put her in the back of the CHP cruiser, she watched Jason drive away in his BMW. She said to the class, "Do you ever look at those video clips on the TV show *Cops* of the person in the back of the police car banging their head against the side window and kicking at the cage between the seats and wonder what would make a person do that? I get it now. I guess I should just be glad no one was videotaping me."

In addition to the DUI, she got a ticket for weaving out of her lane and having a passenger not secured in his seatbelt, which is how she came to traffic school and I got to meet her. Although clearly still angry about several aspects of this, she was not taking it out on me or the class, as often happened.

There were some interesting moments even just during introductions. In reply to my question as to what she did for a living, one woman sort of snarled, "I work for ___ Bank in Santa Monica."

I said, "You don't sound very happy about that."

She said, "I'm not. She went on a little rant about how she used to love her job, but a new person had been transferred in as their branch manager. She said, "This boss used to be at the branch in Marina del Rey and now the Santa Monica branch is stuck with her. Probably because the staff in Marina del Rey couldn't stand her either."

The woman sitting next to the bank employee gave her a piercing look and said, "Did you say you work at the ___ Bank in Santa Monica?"

The first woman seemed a little startled by the question and hesitated before answering, "Yes, why?"

The second woman asked a follow-up question: "Is your manager's name Margaret?" The first woman hesitated a little longer this time before answering, "Yes, why?" "Because Margaret is my sister."

The first woman shook her head ruefully and said, "Well, I was already looking for a new job. I guess that just sped up. A lot."

I always found it fascinating how some classes just aligned. Twenty students: all of them real estate agents or mortgage brokers. Then there was the class of James. There were 13 men in class. No women. The first guy introduced himself as Jim. Then the second guy introduced himself as Jim. Then the third guy said, "Hi, my name is Jim." I said, "Oh, it is not!" He held up his court papers as proof. I said, "This is going to get confusing. Can we call you James?" He said he preferred Jimmy. The next guy said, "I know you're not going to believe me, so here." He handed me his driver's license as proof and added, "Yes, another one. And I do prefer James." The next guy was laughing and said, "You got another James. My friends call me J.T." And so it went as we met James after James, as well as Jimbo and J.P. and Jamie and others. Now with each additional person saying their name was James all we could do was laugh and they felt obligated to offer written proof they were not making this up. We got to the last man and he said, "Yep, me too." I asked what we should call him, and he said he too preferred James. I asked, "You don't have a nickname?" He said, "Not really." I said, "Well what does your wife call you?" He said, "Do you really want to know?" For the rest of the class we all called him *Pookie*.

Why Isn't This a Sitcom?

OFTEN when I would tell people some of my traffic school stories, they asked if I ever thought about making my experiences into a sitcom. As a writer living in Los Angeles, it was hard for me not to think about that. And I wasn't the only one thinking that. Three times I had students who were in the television business ask if they could come back and observe my class a few more times in order to pitch it to a network. A couple of them even promised me that I'd get to be a writer or star of the show if it was picked up.

When they got it together enough to pitch it to a network exec, it always got shot down. The explanation was that very few states had traffic school. Of those that did have it, most only had a serious version for repeat offenders. Few states had the free-wheeling comedy-style classes California did. They did not think most people in the country would be able to relate or get the premise. Most series revolve around a set of characters—the friends on *Friends*, the bar crowd on *Cheers*, the cops on a million police dramas. In traffic school, only the teacher is the constant and that would not give people many recurring characters they could relate to.

Now, traffic school has pretty much gone the way of Blockbuster and porn stores, put out of business by the internet. I stopped teaching when the last schools I worked for shut down as they had too few students to sustain themselves. When I started teaching in 1989, there were something like 900 schools in the state, each one able to fill multiple classes a week with close to 40 students, which was the maximum the DMV allowed. At times the demand for classes so exceeded supply that the DMV would look the other way if there were more than the allowed number. Especially in south Orange County, there was a shortage and I taught a few classes there for more than 60 students. I remember one that I think had 86. I had to call the school to bring me more roll sheets and certificates. They even asked the DMV if we could do it and got permission.

By the time the last school I was working for went under, there were only about 30 brick-and-mortar schools left in the state. Almost everyone was doing class online. We'd be lucky to get eight students in a class and most of them were elderly so didn't know the internet, or were immigrants who barely understood English, which meant the jokes didn't get laughs and there was little fun left for me by then anyway.

Christmas Cheer

WHEN I taught the two-part evening traffic school class, which was 3.5 hours each evening, I encouraged my classes to bring food and have a potluck the second night of class. Most people were coming directly from work, so wouldn't have time to eat. This way if they grabbed something along the way or brought food from home, they could eat in class. I especially liked doing potlucks in the classes I taught in Chula Vista, which has a large population of Filipino and Mexican immigrants and they would often bring heaps of great food and we'd have an international smorgasbord. In other classes, people would chip in for pizza or whatever. At Christmas time, I would encourage parties and people often responded with amazing holiday treats.

One particularly memorable holiday party comes to mind. The second night of class in San Diego, a week or so before Christmas, people outdid themselves. Many dressed for the occasion in Christmas sweaters and Santa hats and reindeer antlers and brought cookies, pies, cakes, candy, and more.

One woman in particular seemed to be having a wonderful time. Laughing, joking, and being overly festive. I had noticed her the night before as she slowly transformed from being dour to laughing, almost a bit too much, at all of my jokes. A woman sitting next to the laughing woman finally said to her in a not-unkind way, "I know the class is fun, and—no offense to Walt—but not *that* funny. What is with you? You haven't stopped laughing since we got here."

The woman said, "I know I'm getting carried away. But I haven't laughed in 14 years."

We all stopped what we were doing and looked at her in shock and puzzlement. Clearly we all wanted more of an explanation, so she went on. "My husband died 14 years ago. And it's not just that he died, it was how he died that yanked the rug out from under my life. If you've been married a long time—we had been married 27 years—you know after a while there are times when you really love your spouse, times you really hate your spouse, and times when you're just kinda indifferent. They're just another piece of furniture you learn to walk around in your life. We were in one of those doldrums. Not fighting, not mad at each other, just bleh. He went off on another business trip. He traveled a lot for business. I took him to the airport and I think the last words I ever said to him were, 'Get out of my car. I'm late.' I didn't yell at him or say it angrily or anything. It was just matter-of-fact. I was late for work and he had started to tell some unimportant story that I knew could wait and I know how antsy the curb cops get at the airport.

"Usually when he got into his hotel, he'd call to say he got in all right and to talk for a minute. But if it was late or he got tied up, he wouldn't wake me just to say hi, so I wasn't surprised or concerned when I didn't get a call that evening. The next morning, I got a call from the El Paso Police saying my husband had been found dead on the floor of his hotel room when the maid came in to clean. He had never even opened his suitcase. An apparent heart attack."

He hadn't been sick or having any medical problems. No history of heart disease. He was 52. The suddenness of it caught her completely unprepared. "We really did have a good marriage. I did love him. I wish I told him that more often. And that it would have been the last thing I said to him."

She said for a while friends tried to get her to come to dinner or a party or go out and she just felt too empty and unsociable to do it. And she found that if you say 'no' often enough to invitations, they stop coming. And that she didn't know where the last 14 years had gone, but she would go to work each day, barely speaking to her coworkers as she went through the motions of her job. She said she was so down at work that people just pretty much left her alone, which they thought was what she wanted.

She'd come home, make and eat dinner, and sit in front of the TV. She said, "I can't even say I watch TV, because I don't even pay attention to what is on. I just sort of stare through the television set. That has been my life for 14 years. No friends, no fun, no laughter. Then an amazing thing happened. I got this ticket. And of course I thought it was horrible, but it turned out to be the best thing that's happened in years. I came to class last night and you people were alive and fun! There is still joy in the world, even in traffic school! I had such a great time last night with all you interesting people. And I laughed. For the first time in years, I laughed, and it felt so good! All the way home last night I was thinking it was the best evening I'd had since my husband died."

By now everyone in the class was tearing up. She continued, "Today, I startled my coworkers by coming in with a smile on my face. I brought donuts for the office and instead of hiding in my office, I carried the box desk to desk to give everybody one and said hello. My boss finally asked what was up and when I told him, he was so happy, he insisted on taking the whole office out to a Christmas lunch to celebrate the new me! I called a friend of mine I hadn't talked to in years. We still exchanged Christmas cards, but that was about it. She and her husband used to always throw a big holiday party, always the Saturday before Christmas. I asked if they still had the party and if I was still welcome to come. She said yes, they would love to see me. I am so excited to start living again. To thank you all, I brought those big things of cookies for tonight and was really looking forward to seeing you all again."

And by now, the whole class was crying and smiling at the same time. I hope she had many more merry days.

The Paramedic's Story of Life & Death

I met many interesting people in my traffic school classes and learned a great deal from lots of them. One of the most powerful lessons came from a guy in a class in San Diego. One day as we went around the room with each student stating their name, their occupation, and what their ticket was for, the part of the class you may remember that I called, *What's Your Name, Who's Your Daddy*, a man said he designed and made custom furniture. But he added, until a few years earlier he had been a paramedic for L.A. County and he had something he wanted to say, if he may. He said it concerned safe driving. And more.

He said he always wanted to be a firefighter/paramedic. He said you get used to things like the sadness of watching people lose everything in a house fire. But the thing he could never get used to was watching people die. That even calling them firefighters was almost a misnomer. "We were really the wrecking crew. Most of our calls were responding to traffic accidents. And in far too many, someone died."

He said all of those people had something in common. Not one woke up that morning thinking, "Today is the day I'll die. No one thinks that. If they did, there is no way they'd get on the freeway." He was not prepared for the number of people who would die on the ambulance ride with him. No one had made it clear that it would be such a big, emotionally draining part of the job.

Too often in the back of the ambulance the injured person would look up at him and ask, "Am I dying?" Some of his fellow paramedics would try to comfort the person saying, "Hang in there! We're almost at the hospital. You're going to be fine!" But he said if he looked into their eyes and knew they knew it was over, he would tell them the truth. He didn't want the last person they ever spoke to on this earth to lie to them.

After acknowledging that the end was near, they would then often tell him their biggest regret. Some were seemingly small, but for it to be on their mind in those final moments, it must have really mattered to them. After telling one woman that she likely wasn't going to make it, she said, "I always wanted to go to Paris. Ever since I was a little girl. I wanted to stand at the top of the Eiffel Tower. I always figured there'd be a next year to go to Paris. But there is no next year. I'll never see the Eiffel Tower. Well, shit." Then she died.

A man said, "I always wanted to learn to play the piano. When I was a child, my mother wanted me to take lessons and I wouldn't do it. All the time now I wish I had. People at a party who are playing the piano look like they are having such a great time. I guess I'll never learn to play the piano." Then exhaled his last breath.

Another man said to him, "The last thing I said to my wife this morning was 'shut up.' Would you please call her and tell her I'm sorry, that I loved her, and my last thoughts were of her?" The former paramedic said, "I wanted to yell at him, 'What the hell have you been doing for eight hours at work today that you couldn't call and tell her that? You couldn't find two minutes to at least leave a message? And now it's on me to do it?'" And he said of course he promised to do it and did. But it still made him upset that people didn't tidy up after themselves.

One man, knowing he was dying, said, "I haven't spoken to my son in 17 years. Last I heard from him, he was living in San Jose. His name is Tyler. Would you call him and tell him I'm sorry and I love him?" The paramedic said, "I wanted to lift him off the gurney and backhand him. You had 17 years to make this call and now it's up to me?" He said, "But I knew I'd do it. The son cried on the phone for over an hour. But think how much more that call would have meant coming from his father, not some stranger who knew his father for 25 minutes before he died."

One day as he watched yet another person die on the way to the hospital it hit him. If he were dying in the back of ambulance, what would his biggest regret be? And he realized it would be that he spent his adult life watching people die in the back of ambulances and that it was making him sad and unhappy. He asked himself what he'd rather be doing. He always wanted to design and build his own furniture. So he got himself a cabin in eastern, rural San Diego County and now he makes his own creations. He said, "It's a bit of a struggle at times. I don't make anywhere near the money or have any of the benefits I had working for L.A. County, but I'm happy. If I were in the back of that ambulance, I would have no regrets."

He turned around to the rest of the class and said, "None of them expected to die that day. Chances are, neither will you when your day comes. So if there is someone you need to talk to, someone you need to apologize to, someone you need to tell you love them, do it. Today. There may not be another chance. If you want to learn to play the piano, or go to Paris, or reconnect with someone, do it. Now."

It is a life lesson I've not forgotten.

One of several displays in the Baseball Hall of Fame at Cooperstown celebrating Pittsburgh Pirate great, and one of the first five players inducted into the Hall, Honus Wagner, to whom my father had a special connection.

VI.
Writing Adventures

M Y writing often gave me interesting opportunities. A few such stories:

Six Degrees from Gettysburg

S INCE writing an earlier version of this essay that appeared in the Pittsburgh Post-Gazette in time for the 150th Anniversary of the Battle of Gettysburg, I have met several other people whose ancestors were in that small Pennsylvania town during early July, 1863.

What prompted this reflection for my hometown newspaper was being at a party in La Jolla, California, hosted by a friend who is a professor at UCSD. Someone brought up the movie Gettysburg. Given how much I like that movie I wanted to join that discussion. As many times as I have seen that epic movie, my heart still races when Jeff Daniels, as Joshua Lawrence Chamberlain, orders his troops to fix bayonets and charge. Even though I should know by now how that episode comes out, I still find myself yelling at the TV, "Don't do it, Josh! It's suicide!" Seeing that movie had me intrigued enough by Chamberlain, that I went out of my way in Maine to go to Bowdoin College and see his home, his Medal of Honor, his boots, and sword.

At the discussion of the movie in La Jolla, one of the guests, Joel Nimon, said he was always interested in Gettysburg because one of the landmarks on that battlefield, the Spangler farm, had belonged to his family during the Civil War.

I found this interesting, since in doing extensive research on a novel I'm writing set in and around Gettysburg during and after the battle, I'd come across numerous references to the ancestors of people I've met.

The soldiers who faced off in Gettysburg just bumped into each other as well. Generals Robert E. Lee and George Meade had each planned a different site for the confrontation they both knew was coming. But because all of the roads in that part of Pennsylvania came together in Gettysburg, their armies stumbled across each other and the largest battle ever fought in North America was joined. Not only did all roads lead to Gettysburg, but the convergence of people that occurred there echoes down to the present day.

I wrote this original essay in a San Diego coffee shop owned by John Husler. Husler's great-great-grandfather, Major General Winfield Scott Hancock, commanded the Second Corps in the Battle of Gettysburg.

Although severely wounded during the repulse of Pickett's Charge, Hancock refused to be removed from the field until he was sure his Union troops had prevailed. Hancock came from eastern Pennsylvania: he was born in Philadelphia and raised in Norristown. In 1880 he ran for president against James Garfield, but his old wound pained him so much he refused to campaign, rarely leaving his front porch, and he still barely lost the election. In another connection that loops back around, my sister later worked for Rudolph Garfield, the great-grand-son of President Garfield.

My father worked at Mellon Bank in Pittsburgh with a man named Alexander Hays, IV. Alex's great-great grandfather, for whom he was named, Brigadier General Alexander Hays (the first) commanded the First Brigade of the Third Division of Hancock's Second Corps. I found it an interesting coincidence that I knew two people whose ancestors had known each other so well and worked so closely together at Get-

The statue of General Alexander Hays at Gettysburg.

tysburg (and in other engagements throughout the war).

There is a story that before the Battle, Hancock had cursed out one of Hays' officers and after the battle, he said to Hays, "I guess I ought to apologize to him." Hays replied, "That's just like all of your damned apologies, Hancock. They come too late. He's dead."

My father knew of General Hays, having heard about him a few times from his co-worker. Knowing my interest in the Civil War, my father got me an invite to the Hays family home in Sewickley, which had a shrine to the general's memory. The general was killed while leading his troops at the Battle of the Wilderness in 1864. There is a large memorial on his grave in Allegheny Cemetery and there are smaller memorial plaques to his memory elsewhere in Western Pennsylvania.

At the entrance to Gettysburg National Military Park, a statue of General Hays welcomes you, his sword and bushy beard both heroically projecting out in front him. Hays' troops took much of the brunt of Pickett's Charge and his statue recognizes that. Hays' Brigade captured the flags of over 20 Confederate regiments that broke apart in front of his lines. After Pickett's Charge had been repulsed, Hays gathered up several of the captured Confederate colors and rode up and down the Union line, trailing the flags in the dust as the soldiers in blue cheered.

My father wasn't as familiar with the Battle as I have become, so the last name of his parish priest didn't ring a bell. I had met the priest a few times in passing, but only as Father Joe. I didn't learn his last name when I met him, or I'm sure I would have asked him about the possible Gettysburg connection. Knowing my interest, my father told me as soon as he learned of it.

One day my father was in Father Joe's office and heard someone ask the priest if he was any relation to the Codori family of Gettysburg. The priest answered that was indeed his family. The Codori house still stands in the middle of the battlefield, not far from the Spangler farm. Those two farms have served as reference points for historians and tourists since the Battle.

On July 2, 1863, the second day of the three-day battle, General Hays went to General Hancock and asked for permission to burn the houses and barns that were obstructing his field of fire and being used as cover by Confederate snipers. Among the buildings he wanted to remove were those of the Codori farm. Early in the war, before General Sherman made war on civilians an art form, there was an attempt to avoid damaging private property unless absolutely necessary.

After assessing the situation, Hancock agreed to the military necessity of removing the buildings. Hays ordered infantry companies forward to wrest the houses and barns from the Confederate soldiers occupying them and burn the structures to the ground. Several buildings were burned, but the troops failed to capture the Codori farm. The buildings were heavily damaged by shot and shell and bullets, but they survive to this day, their scars bearing mute testimony to the fighting.

The lives of Hays, Hancock, and Codori converged on that field, and now, a century and a half later, I knew the descendants of all three. My great-great-grandfather was also present that day wearing blue. Thomas Donahue shows up on the roster of the 28th Pennsylvania volunteers, but given his lowly rank and his unit's position guarding a supply train away from the thick of the fighting, I doubt he ever encountered the more notable names from the Battle. My great-aunt went to the 75th anniversary commemoration in Gettysburg in 1938 and I have the medallion she brought back from that celebration in honor of her grandfather. I also have a bullet that she picked up on the battlefield. When she was young, such artifacts were still readily found and it wasn't yet illegal to pick them up.

Many other Americans can trace their family trees across that Battlefield as well. General George S. Patton's great-great-uncle was killed fighting for Virginia in Pickett's Charge, and President Richard Nixon's great-grandfather died at Gettysburg fighting for the Union.

Over the years, I have met a Booth and a Lee, both of whom said their families included the Booths and Lees, who figured prominently in Civil War history. Actor Tom Hanks is related to Abraham Lincoln's mother, Nancy Hanks.

A friend of mine from my Penn State days had been married to his wife for years before they discovered that each had a great-great-grandfather who fought for the Union and who had escaped the notorious prison camp at Andersonville, Georgia.

At the Battle of Malvern Hill in 1862, the Timberlake Store figured as a focal point. Given what an unusual last name that is, I am curious if Justin's ancestors owned a store in Virginia back then.

Actor Matthew Broderick's great-great-grandfather fought at Gettysburg and survived, but was not as fortunate in the battle for Atlanta a year later. Broderick starred in the Civil War movie "Glory". He also appeared in *She's Having a Baby* with Kevin Bacon, who is from an old Philadelphia family. I read that Private Elijah W. Bacon, Company F, won the Medal of Honor at Gettysburg. I wonder...

Kevin Bacon is married to actress Kyra Sedgwick. Kyra's ancestor,

General John Sedgwick was also at Gettysburg. He was killed in the Battle of Spotsylvania a year later, just four days after General Hays was killed at the Wilderness.

On a visit to my brother, he took me to tour the L.T. Moore house in Winchester, Virginia. The home was owned by Confederate Lieutenant-Colonel Moore of a Virginia regiment, who loaned it to General Stonewall Jackson to use as his headquarters while fighting in the area. When the historic home fell into disrepair, donations were solicited to restore the home and a large chunk of money came from the lieutenant-colonel's great-granddaughter, Mary Tyler Moore.

(Side note about my brief crossing of paths with Matthew Broderick. When I lived in Venice, California, I used to often ride the beach bike path. It was a beautiful ride along the sand, stretching from Santa Monica down to Torrance. I would try to take my rides pretty early in the day before the path became too crowded, which could get dangerous. Sometimes I would find myself in an undeclared race with another rider. Riders would just start dueling without saying a word. The faster riding made for a better workout.

One day I had fallen into racing another bike. We never said a word, we just started going faster and faster side by side. We were flying along and came to the sharp turns where the bike path cuts out toward the ocean to zig around the Scattergood Power Plant. There, closer to the water, sand had drifted up onto the bike path and was several inches deep on the concrete. We were on bicycles meant for riding on streets; they didn't have the thick tires of beach cruisers or mountain bikes. If we went into that deep sand at high speed, the narrow front wheel would stop, and we'd be flying face-first over the handlebars.

Without saying a word, by tacit agreement, my racing rival and I each decided to lay our bikes down in kind of controlled crashes, sliding sideways off the bike path, him to the left, me to the right. Once we had both come to a stop, he looked up and said, "Are you ok?" I said I was and asked about him. He and his bike were also fine. We each dusted ourselves off, picked up our bicycles and began to portage them over the sand. We made small talk as we did, still not acknowledging that we had been racing. I kept looking at him and trying to place the face and voice. He looked very familiar. But I couldn't quite figure out how I knew him. When we got to where the bike path was clear again, he put down his bicycle, jumped on and sped off, trying to get a head start on his competition.

I was left flatfooted holding my bike as it registered why the guy looked so familiar! It was Ferris Bueller himself! Matthew Broderick! Now I really tried to speed up to catch him. It would have been great to actually meet him. But he had such a jump on me, and was a fast rider, so I never did. I barely could even keep him in sight.

Oh well, life moves pretty fast. If you don't stop and look around once in a while, you could miss it.)

The Deacon

FOR a piece I wrote for the website *Baseball Savvy* I got the chance to interview Pittsburgh Pirate great, and one of my boyhood heroes, Vernon Law.

Shortly before I was to speak to him, I was working on the television pilot for the TV version of my stage play, *GAM3RS*, and somehow it came up that I was going to be talking to Law in a few days. One of the actresses in the show said, "Oh wow! Tell Vern I said hi!" I was surprised she knew him. Turns out he coached baseball at the high school in Provo, Utah and two of her brothers had played for him. Her family had known him for years.

I was in Pittsburgh visiting my parents when it came the appointed time to interview the baseball legend. They asked who I was interviewing now and when I told them, it was fun to watch my father, a big Pirate and Law fan, turn into a jealous 6-year-old. "How come you get to talk to Vern Law? I wanna talk to Vern Law!" My father had taken me to see Law, Clemente, Maz, and the other legendary Pirates play at Forbes Field.

I started my conversation with Law by saying, "Amy Ashworth says hi."

He was a little startled by that and asked, "How do you know Amy?"

It's always good to establish rapport with an interview subject. It set the stage for a great talk.

Law told me that he might be the only man in the history of major league baseball to be booted out of a game because of someone else's bad language. He claims it was Nellie King, sitting next to him, who was hollering bad things that Law never would. The ump came over to the dugout and said, "That's it, Law, you're out of here!" Law said, "I was embarrassed to be out there any way with all the bad language." Vern *The Deacon* Law is still fondly remembered in Pittsburgh and baseball circles for his stellar conduct both on and off the field. His nickname isn't quite accurate; he's not really a deacon. "But nobody in Pittsburgh back then really knew what an 'elder' was." Vern is an elder of the Mormon Church.

His part in the most dramatic World Series ending in history is the stuff of legends and is celebrated at the Baseball Hall of Fame in Cooperstown. The Yankees scored more than twice as many runs as the Pirates in that '60 series. These were the Yankees of Maris and Mantle and Berra, with so much firepower that everyone was predicting a New York sweep, but Law pitched well enough for the Bucs to take Game 1 at Pittsburgh's Forbes Field. Law said, "Roy Face came in and finished up that game and he gave up some hits. Same way in New York. I had a 3-2 game going and he came in and gave up some hits." But the Pirates won that one, too. Law was 2-0 in World Series starts.

In the seventh game, the Bucs had the lead when Pirate Manager Danny Murtaugh pulled Law for a relief pitcher as well. Law said, "It was the same in that last game; I went 6 and 2/3rds innings. Murtaugh took me out and brought in Roy Face and Roy couldn't get anybody out, so Hal Smith hits a three-run homer. They bring in (Bob) Friend. The first two guys that face Friend, they get on base. So they bring in Harvey Haddix, and by the time Harvey gets them out, they've scored two runs to tie it up, and then in our half of the 9th inning, Maz hit the homerun to win it." More amazingly, Vern pitched all three of his starts with a taped-up sprained ankle.

Bill Mazeroski's walk-off homer to break the tie in the bottom of the 9th has gone down in history, remembered as perhaps the greatest baseball moment ever.

Vern Law was the last major-leaguer to throw 18 innings in a game (and this on only two days' rest). The Pirates won that one back in 1955, but Bob Friend got the decision. The two most note-worthy games of Law's career—the seventh game of the World Series and that one—Law started, did his job superbly and then was left out of many of the write-ups because he was not the pitcher of record. He had the most complete games of any pitcher in 1960 and picked up the Cy Young Award.

It was fun talking to Vern Law. And I thought it was great that I was now two degrees of separation from some of the greatest ballplayers of all time: Mickey Mantle, Jackie Robinson, Roberto Clemente, and so many others.

One of the last things my Dad and I did together before he was too ill to go out was to go to see Yankees at PNC Park. It was the first time the team with the pinstripes had played in Pittsburgh since the momentous 1960 Series. Interleague play allowed for this rare match-up. My father and I enjoyed seeing the Bucs beat the Yankees. It was a fitting end to my father's years of following the Pirates. As a teen, my father had a job selling programs at Forbes Field and was there when Babe Ruth hit his last homeruns. The Bambino hit three balls out of the park in the final plate appearances of his career, helping to defeat the Pirates, but I don't think my father minded seeing the 39-year-old legend go out with a bang.

My father was not aware of it at the time, but his future brother-in-law was also at that game. My father would not even meet my mother for another 14 years, but my maternal grandfather and his brother took their two sons to that fateful game. My grandfather and my great-uncle were a couple of charmers, both made their livings as salesmen, and they could talk just about anyone into just about anything. They some-how managed to wheedle their way into the locker room of the Boston Braves (for whom the Babe was playing in his final season). They asked the Babe to sign a baseball for each of their boys and he obliged. Sadly, they did not use a very good pen and didn't know how to protect the balls, and now, 85 years later, the autographs are so faded it's hard to tell there is even ink on them and it's not even remotely possible to see whose name it was. My uncle at some point had his ball appraised and the answer was that it's worthless. Anything he might do to try to en-hance the signature would negate its value. Without some sort of proof that the Babe signed it, it's just another old baseball.

My Dad had seen other legends play including some of the Pirate greats and future Hall of Famers: Pie Traynor and the Waner Broth-ers—Big Poison and Little Poison—one of only two sets of brothers enshrined in Cooperstown.

When I finally made it to visit the baseball Hall of Fame in Cooper-stown, I was surprised and pleased how much of the Hall is devoted to Pirate history. Cooperstown is not near anything, so as much as I wanted to visit it for a long time, I just could never find the time to journey out from New York City or Erie, Pennsylvania, the only places I ever went that were anywhere near the remote, picturesque village. While visiting a friend in Oneonta, it was an easy 30-minute drive. I am very glad I went. The town itself is pretty and quaint and the HoF is a must-see for baseball fans.

Not surprisingly, the Hall is heavy on Yankees who have won more series and had more legendary players than any other team. But I didn't expect how much space was devoted to the Pirates. I didn't count or measure, but if I had to guess, I would say about 40 percent of the Hall is Yankees, 25 percent Pirates, and the remaining 35 percent split among all of the other teams past and present. Of course, Honus Wagner was there; he was one of the first five players inducted into the HoF. For years, my father worked with Honus's daughter Virginia, so he has a special place in our hearts. And Roberto Clemente—whole books are written about his greatness on and off the field, so I won't try to do him justice here. I had seen him play. And Willie Stargell and the *We Are Family* team that won the 1979 series.

One thing about that 1979 Pirate team: they were the first all-Black team since the Negro Leagues. Depending on who was pitching (they did have some white pitchers and a few other replacement fielders), their standard team was all African Americans. That is why to this day you often see older African Americans wearing Pirate caps, especially older folks who remember that season. That team was sort of adopted as the national Black team, as the *Pittsburgh Courier* once was sort of the Black *USA Today* and had the largest circulation of any newspaper serving the Black community. It is one of the oldest African-American newspapers in the country and pre-television was seen as the source of news all across the country.

Speaking of the Negro Leagues, Pittsburgh was the only city to field two teams in that league: The Homestead Grays and Pittsburgh Crawfords. There is now a bridge in the city named for those teams and the City of Bridges, as Pittsburgh likes to bill itself, also has a Bridge named for Roberto Clemente; appropriately enough, it leads to the current ballpark.

The HoF also has exhibits about Forbes Field and Maz and the 1960 World Series. It was fun to see the Pirates enshrined so out of proportion to their number of World Series victories.

I had never seen that famous 1960 World Series Game 7, nor had most people. Games were not televised in the city in which they were played, and they were not routinely recorded as they are today. Anyone who didn't catch the game live had no way to see that historic moment. That was the case until a year after my father died.

A kinescope recording of the game was found in Bing Crosby's wine cellar. That might seem an unlikely place to find such valuable footage, but the story actually makes sense. The famous crooner was a part owner of the Pirates back then. His buddy Bob Hope owned a piece of the Cleveland Browns. Crosby thought the idea of the Pirates winning the Series would be too much to handle in person, so he went to Europe. But he did want to see the game, so he hired someone to record it. The recordings were forgotten about until someone was cleaning out Crosby's cellar. Apparently he had stored them in the dark, dry, cold environment to help protect them.

Crosby was not the only one the game was going to drive crazy. Arrangements were made for EPSN films to create a DVD of the game. I bought a copy and took it to Pittsburgh to watch with my mother. She, like many others, had listened to the game on the radio, but had never seen it. The game had special significance for her.

My grandmother's sister and brother-in-law, my great-aunt and uncle, went to a couple of the games. I have their ticket stubs from Game 1 and alsoSthat crucial Game 7. My grandmother didn't want to go with them for fear she wouldn't be able to handle the excitement. While listening as the radio announcers called Maz's homer, my grandmother had a heart attack. She survived that heart attack. When the Pirates were next in the Series, 1971, against the Orioles, she had another heart attack from which she never fully recovered and died the following spring. She did love her Bucs, so it was not an unfitting ending to her life.

I had only heard about the finale of that seventh game, but on the video it was fun to watch a great see-saw contest with a lot of great plays and excitement. Having heard from Vern Law how much he argued with his manager not to be removed from the game, I could see in his body language his reluctance to give up the ball and leave the mound. Although we obviously knew the outcome of the game, my Mother and I got caught up in the growing excitement, wondering how the lowly Buccos could possibly pull out a victory against the mighty Yankees.

The Yankees scored more than twice as many runs as the Pirates in the series. The Pirates were winning games 6-4, 3-2 and 5-2 while the boys in pinstripes were winning their games in blowouts 16-3, 10-0, 12-0. The Bucs were squeaking out wins while the Yankees were romping in theirs. There was no way the upstart Pirates could pull this out. But somehow they did and the excitement was all on film.

The other thing my mother and I found fascinating in watching the game was how much things surrounding the actual game had changed. Of course the game was shot in black and white. Now we are used to a hundred camera angles in the World Series, when everyone but the batboy has a camera trained on them at all times, but back then there might have been six cameras to cover the whole game.

The other thing that seemed so different were the shots of the stands. There were hardly any women present. The crowd looked to be 75 percent or more male. And dress has certainly changed for attendance at sporting events. The women present were all in dresses and the vast majority of the men were in suits and ties with wide-brimmed fedoras. And almost everyone was smoking cigarettes.

One last story about baseball and my parents. On one of my visits to Pittsburgh, I brought a copy of the movie *61** to watch with them. A friend of mine played a batboy in the movie, although all of his lines and most of his scenes ended up on the cutting room floor. His role was reduced to blink-and-you-miss-him moments. The movie covers the race in 1961 between Mickey Mantle and Roger Maris to break Babe Ruth's record of 60 homeruns in a season. Knowing how much my parents liked that era of baseball, I thought they would enjoy the movie. In an attempt to show how saintly Maris was and what a cad Mantle was off the field, the movie shows "The Mick" drinking and swearing a lot.

After we watched the movie, my mother wanted my father and me to hang a set of drapes. We were standing on chairs doing that chore while discussing the film. My mother almost startled both of us off our chairs when she said, "I'd have liked the movie better if Mickey Mantle hadn't said *motherfucker* quite so much." I don't think either my Dad or I had ever heard her use that word. After I caught myself and my breath, I told her that her point was well taken, "They shouldn't have had Mickey swear so much, we'd have gotten the point with a lot less vulgarity and the movie might have been suitable for children to learn a valuable lesson about worshipping false heroes." And I added that I would be very happy to never hear her use that word again. Once was too much.

ANOTHER fun opportunity my writing afforded me…

Taking It to the Ice

SINCE I was about seven years old and saw my first Zamboni at a Pittsburgh Penguins game, I wanted to ride one. I think anyone who has been to an ice arena has had that childish desire. Most people never outgrow it. Back in 2006, thanks to the San Diego Gulls hockey team and their long-time Zamboni driver, Ralph Bedoe, I got my wish. I had been writing about the Gulls for a local website and used that as an excuse to wangle a ride.

I took the opportunity to talk to Ralph about his job, the Zamboni, and the public's fascination with it. "The hype goes away right when you get on it and you realize it's just a machine that you're driving around," Bedoe says, and he's right. After one lap of the ice I got it. It's not a very exciting route they drive. I'm really glad I did it, but if I never got to ride one again, my life would not be poorer for it.

Bedoe sees his job as two-fold: entertainment and cutting the ice. He has a few different looks he sports for his drive around the ice—he chauffeured me around while wearing a bushy wig. He waves to the crowd and mixes up his route to the amusement of season ticket holders who know what pattern he should be following. Usually a child is selected to ride shotgun on the Zamboni, and he also feels it's his duty to make sure his passenger is having a good time. He entertained me with stories as we made our circuit.

He noted the fascination many people have for his vehicle. Zamboni groupies have waited for him at the end of his run and people have put signs up for him, including one that read, "Zamboni driver, I want to have your love child."

He said. "Typically, after an event and I'm cleaning the ice and people are leaving the Arena Club, girls come out of the club and get out to the entrance of the ice and they see me out there, they want to get on the Zamboni and ride it around." He has been married since he's been doing this job, so he has never availed himself of the many offers he gets.

Bedoe says it takes concentration to make sure he doesn't miss a spot or that he doesn't lay down too much water. On one occasion he was so distracted that he made a rare miscue. The distraction: He got flashed. "Every time I would pass by this girl, she acted like she was going to pull her top up. About the third time I went down, she did pull her top up and of course, I screwed up 'cause I lost my concentration. I left a spot that I had to go back and get."

He has also had one of his passengers flash the crowd: "I had a rider who worked at a local strip club flash the audience. She got kicked out 'cause it's a family thing and they don't want that to happen. I was paying attention to the turns, so I wasn't able to observe. I only heard about it after it happened." Cheap thrills aside, there is serious work to be done. He has a limited time to finish his job, so can't be messing around or making too many repeat passes. Bedoe estimated he has done over 2000 "cuts" as the cleaning of the ice is called. That is really what the machine does: slices off a layer of ice and then lays down a fresh layer of water which should, if applied properly, freeze almost instantly.

Getting the perfect cut, however, isn't as easy as it often looks. The tray that's dragged behind the Zamboni is called a conditioner, and inside the conditioner there's a 72-inch blade that cuts the ice. "When I go out there between periods to cut the ice, I have to back the blade off, because if I were to get all of the ice from their skates, plus shave the ice, it would fill the Zamboni up and I'd have to come back. It's kind of tricky and the first couple times you have to really pay attention to how much snow you're picking up. Old-school machines were even more fun to watch with their seemingly endless supply of snowballs. After the cut ice is removed, the back part of the conditioner has a large towel called a "spreader" that lays down the water coat.

The ice is only 3/4ths of an inch to an inch thick, which doesn't leave much room for error. If the ice is too thin, a skate could cut through to the concrete underneath. If it's too thick, the ice on top is too far from the cooling coils and could get soft. The ice surface is kept 16-18 degrees Fahrenheit for hockey, but 24-25 degrees for figure skating. The figure skaters like it softer so they can plant to do their jumps and turns. Hockey players, however, want it harder so the puck will skim over the surface faster and they can move faster. Another reason is that with so many players on the ice at once, softer ice would quickly get chewed up.

Everyone should get to ride a Zamboni once, for as the great twentieth century American philosopher Charlie Brown once observed in the comic strip *Peanuts*, "There are three things in life that people like to stare at: A rippling stream, a crackling fire and a Zamboni clearing the ice."

A rainbow above the mountains of Michoacán, Mexico.

VII.
The
Coming Out
Ring

EVERY year since my friend Bill had committed suicide, his mother and I had exchanged Christmas cards. I'm one of those people who does holiday letters. As I have drifted apart from college friends, those annual missives are the only updates I get or give to them and some others in my life, including Bill's mother. In the holiday letter of 1997, I had announced to the world that after years of hiding the truth even from myself, I had finally come to terms with being gay.

I had just moved to the Normal Heights neighborhood of San Diego from where I had been living in northern San Diego County. The house that I was now renting was on the hill above the Qualcomm Stadium where the 1998 Super Bowl would be held, close enough to hear the blimp engines and to walk out to my front porch to see the Blue Angels' flyover and watch the fireworks show. I decided to throw a Super Bowl/house-warming/coming-out party.

When I packed for the move, I had vowed I would really weed things out. If I was never going to read that book or wear that shirt again, I'd donate it. Bags of clothes went to Goodwill and boxes of books went to the library.

The Friday before Super Bowl Sunday, I still had lots of unpacking to do and I had promised myself that every single box would be emptied so I'd have Saturday free for party prep. I had about 15 boxes to go and was slicing into them, quickly dispatching whatever I found to the appropriate shelf, closet, or cabinet. Then it happened. I slit open a box that I moved to Carlsbad and from Carlsbad without having ever opened. It had stayed for years out of sight up above my car on the joists of the garage. I knew I was never going to wear the clothes that were in it or read the books or look at the photos hidden in it.

In it were all of the things that reminded me of Bill. Photos of the trips we had taken together, music cassettes, books, clothes, and gifts he had given me over the years of our friendship. Shortly after Bill's death, unable to deal with my guilt and sadness, I had sealed all remembrances of him away and had no intention of opening that box, either before or after the move.

I've lost close friends to cancer and felt terrible, but I never felt guilty. I can't cure cancer. Suicide is different. I couldn't have done anything to prevent the car accidents that claimed other friends' lives.

But suicide, rightly or wrongly, feels preventable. If I had listened better, if I had been a better friend, maybe it wouldn't have happened. Bill's suicide haunted me so badly that I couldn't bear to think about him without it causing days of depression.

When I opened that box, I saw on top a bicycling jersey Bill had given me. It made my heart sink. I hadn't planned to deal with this box now or ever, but in my haste to finish unpacking, I had attacked the box without reading the magic marker warning on the top. Shit. I didn't have time to deal with this. But the jersey wouldn't release my stare. I had way too much to do and couldn't spend time fixating on a stupid shirt. I should just re-seal the box and get back to work.

Then I remembered my self-imposed dictum to get rid of anything I would never wear again. But I couldn't throw the shirt out. It was one of my last tangible reminders of Bill. A reminder I couldn't bring myself to even look at, let alone wear, so I should just donate it to Goodwill. But I couldn't give it away. I should just seal the box and deal with it another time. But I had to deal with it sometime. I should just throw it out. And so it went, my wheels spinning in the same circle as I faced what I had avoided for years. I also thought of the absurdity of keeping a cycling jersey—my knees were too shot to ride more than a mile or two anyway. My days of riding centuries were over; that was something else Bill and I had in common, our knees had curtailed our ability to cycle 100 miles or more in a day.

I got tired of standing over the box, but still couldn't let go of the dilemma. I carried the shirt to the living room and held it as I sat and stared at it and replayed the options in my head. Donate it. I can't. Wear it. I can't. Only to dismiss them all and start over again. After at least an hour, maybe two, I grew tired of my stupid indecision. I needed to go pick up my mail from my P.O. box before they closed and I hadn't put a shirt on yet that day, so I just decided, screw it. It's just a shirt. Put it on and go get the mail.

In that day's mail was a package slip. I stood in line and gave it to the clerk who retrieved a padded envelope just slightly too large to fit in the box. On it was Bill's mother's return address. A month earlier, I had already received my once-a-year communication from her—a card with the usual short note, something to the effect of, "I hope you're doing well"—so I hadn't expected anything.

With great curiosity, I opened the envelope. In it was a gold ring. I recognized it immediately as Bill's. He treasured that ring and had worn it for years. It had been made for him by his great-uncle, a dentist in England who used scraps of dental gold in wax molds to make jewelry of his own designs. After Bill's great-uncle's death, the ring meant even more to him as a daily reminder of the man who had been his surrogate grandfather. Bill and I had that in common, also—we each had a special great-uncle who took the place of the grandfathers we both lacked.

After one trip to England to visit his mother's family, Bill came back heartbroken. He said he had been helping his mother's brother work in the garden and in the course of the digging and planting apparently the ring had slipped off his wet and slimy finger. He didn't notice it was gone until they were done and he was washing his hands. They went back to the garden and raked and dug and searched. They even borrowed a metal detector, but to no avail. Bill had lost the last piece of his great-uncle and there was no way to replace it.

In the package with Bill's ring was a handwritten note from his mother. She said her brother had been working in his garden and found the ring. He thought she should have it. She received the ring the same day she got my coming out letter and she knew I had to have the ring. She said she was giving it to me by proxy for Bill and that she was happy that I had finally found the self-acceptance that Bill never had. Suddenly everything fell into place. The real reason Bill had killed himself.

I sat in the car and cried until I calmed down enough to drive home. It also seemed beyond coincidence that for the first time since Bill had died, I was wearing a shirt he had given me—while I was holding his ring.

Bill's death had always been a scab for me. Not an open wound, but a barely-healed scab over a wound I was afraid to go anywhere near for fear of causing damage too deep to handle. I had a hard time ever remembering the good times with Bill since the ending was so horrible and my guilt so overwhelming that I shut out thinking about him at all. With the ring, I felt like he had forgiven me (if there was ever anything to forgive) and I knew I could finally start to think of him without immediately going to the bad places.

When I got home, I called a friend of Bill's in L.A. and asked how soon I could see him. Monday, the day after the Super Bowl, I drove to L.A. to have dinner with him. He and Bill had gone to high school together and lived together in Belgium for almost a year when they were trying to break into the ranks of professional track cyclists. I figured if anyone knew if Bill was secretly gay, this

Bill, our mutual friend, and me on a trip to San Francisco.

friend would. He said that even in high school, Bill's friends had assured him that it was okay to come out. He'd still be their friend, and it would be okay. But Bill always vehemently denied being gay.

I asked why he thought Bill was gay and he ran through a list of stereotypical gay interests, including liking Morrissey, Lucy, and Marilyn Monroe. The way he dressed and held his cigarette. I had noticed some of those things, but attributed the mannerism to being half-English, and spending so much time in Europe. (There is the old joke: Is he gay? No, just European.) The friend also said he wondered about my friendship with Bill and how quickly Bill and I became friends when we started working together, and Bill at times saying things about me that crossed the line from friendship to crush.

The talk helped me understand so much. In my mind I replayed many of the moments I'd had with Bill and they made so much more sense now.

Once I sorted out the flood of emotions, I wrote to his mother and told her that far more than his ring, she had given me back Bill. I know Bill is still with me. He is a part of me and I can enjoy the good memories without having to dwell on the bad. I cried for days when he died, but had been afraid to since; afraid to start again for fear I'd never stop. I finally let out what I had kept inside. It put one more piece of my old unhappy life behind me, to be even happier out of the closet.

I was able to unpack the rest of the box of Bill's stuff. Wear those shirts again. Look at photos of him and display some of the other gifts he had given me.

Years later, I sent Bill's mother her annual Christmas card and a few days later got an email from a real estate agent in Pasadena. He said he was sorry to inform me that Bill's mother had died. He said in addition to selling the house for her family in England, he had been asked to check mail and follow up on things that required it. Bill's mother never got over the death of her only son so at least now she was at peace.

I am still weirded out by the coincidence of the timing, but there has to be a message here. If I ever needed a final endorsement that I was doing the right thing by choosing to be happy for the first time in my life, Bill's ring was certainly it. I wish he could have found the same happiness.

Bill's ring on my hand.

I have had so many people ask about the ring over the years. Sometimes just holding out my credit card to pay in a store, the clerk has grabbed my hand and wanted to look at the ring. Some seemed to sense there was a magic to it and asked if it had a story. Once at a drugstore, I started telling the story to the clerk and then I realized a line was forming at the register. I apologized to the people in line and stepped aside so everyone else in the line could pay and they all protested, "No, this is good. Go on. Finish the story. Please continue." And I told them the story of Bill and the ring.

Coming in Volume 2

If You Weren't Here
This Would Not be Happening

~More odd jobs
~Adventures while writing
~ More True Tales from Traffic School
~1984 L.A. Olympics
~The Barcelona Olympics and travels in Europe
~More travels in Mexico
~More tales of life & death
~The adventures of the "Traveling Angel"

The author speaking at an event at the San Diego History Center.

Walter G. Meyer is the co- or ghost-writer of six nonfiction books including *The Respectful Leader*, an Amazon-best-selling and Axiom Award-winning business fable. His critically-acclaimed, award-winning, and Amazon-bestselling novel *Rounding Third* deals powerfully with the topic of teens being bullied. It was published just before the bullying crisis started making the news and he created a presentation *Accept and Respect: the keys to ending bullying*, which he has taken to colleges, high schools, and corporations across the country. He has been on radio and television programs including NPR and he has spoken at colleges, libraries and community centers across the country.

Mr. Meyer's articles have appeared in *Kiplinger's Personal Finance, The Los Angeles Times, Orange County Register, Westways, Baja Explorer, Out, The Pittsburgh Post-Gazette* and dozens of other magazines and newspapers. He is the co-author of a widely-produced stage play *GAM3RS*, which led to him co-creating *Gam3rCon*, a gaming convention built around the play. Several of his screenplays have been optioned, but never quite made into movies--yet.

To support his writing habit over the years he has worked a variety of jobs, some of which are chronicled in his plogs. He began writing his plogs during the Covid quarantine, publishing them one story at a time on Facebook to entertain himself and his friends and followers.

Originally from Pittsburgh, Mr. Meyer has a degree from the School of Communications at Penn State and currently resides in San Diego.

Thank you to:

My editor and head cheerleader, Cindy Burnham.

Zach Bunshaft for additional edits and going on so many new adventures with me.

Eric Shanower for additional artwork.

The many Facebook readers who offered encouragement and advice and support along the way.

Key to front cover

Above the title: Random slides, photos, and contact sheets.

Below the word *This*: bronze medallion my great-aunt Jean brought back from the commemoration of the 75th Anniversary of the Battle of Gettysburg in honor of her grandfather who fought there, against the background of a photo of cannon at Gettysburg. (See: Six Degrees of Gettysburg in Section VI.)

Below *Not Be*: Ticket stubs from Games 1 & 7 of the 1960 World Series. (See: The Deacon I Section VI.)

Under *Happening*: San Diego Public Library Local Author medal against the background of Walt about to take off in a biplane. (See: Chapter One.)

Down the left side below the Gettysburg medallion: Bolo tie with the 14th Air Force logo. (See: My First Close Call in Hollywood in Section IV.)

Photo of Walt riding a Zamboni. (See: Taking it to the Ice in Section VI.)

Gold ring. (See: The Coming Out Ring in Section VII.)

Photo of Walt with Shirley Jones. (See: Shirley You Can't Be Serious in Section IV.)

Made of Awesome button. (See: reference to *GAM3RS* in The Deacon in Section VI.)

Medallion from the 1994 World Cup. (See: He Can't Go Home, They'll Kill Him in Section II.)

Down the Center below the World Series Tickets:
Walt's ID card from Santa Monica College. (See: *Tales from the Darkside* in Section IV.)

Mexican Coin. (See: Memories of Michoacán in Section III.)

Photo of the hermit of Desengueño. (See: The Hermit of Desengueño in Section III.)

Miniature Pennsylvania License Plate. (See: Hooray for Hollywood in Section IV.)

Photo of Walt digging turtle nests. (See: Memories of Michoacán in Section III.)

Below the Post-It note: Photo of a ponga on the Sea of Cortez. (See: Adventures in Baja in Section III.)

On the right side below the biplane photo: Button with a leatherback turtle. (See: Memories of Michoacán in Section III.)

Contact sheet of black & white photos of Mexico.

Opposite page: Sergio and his dog, Cabo Pulmo, Baja California, Mexico. This photo was used on notecards that were sold in gift shops all over Baja.

CPSIA information can be obtained
at www.ICGtesting.com
Printed in the USA
BVHW022144190322
631948BV00023B/456